Stories of God at Home

A Godly Play Approach

Jerome W. Berryman

Church Publishing
NEW YORK

To Thea
as always,
and to families
everywhere

Church Publishing
19 East 34th Street
New York, NY 10016
www.churchpublishing.org

Cover design by Jennifer Kopec, 2Pug Design
Layout and typesetting by Beth Oberholtzer

Library of Congress Cataloging-in-Publication Data

Names: Berryman, Jerome, author.
Title: Stories of God at home : a godly play approach / Jerome W. Berryman.
Description: New York : Church Publishing, 2018. |
Identifiers: LCCN 2017052050 (print) | LCCN 2018006520 (ebook) | ISBN
    9780898690507 (ebook) | ISBN 9780898690491 (pbk.)
Subjects: LCSH: Families—Religious life. | Storytelling—Religious aspects—Christianity. |
    Christian education of children. | God (Christianity)
Classification: LCC BV4526.3 (ebook) | LCC BV4526.3 .B47 2018 (print) | DDC
    249—dc23
LC record available at https://lccn.loc.gov/2017052050

Printed in the United States of America

Contents

Acknowledgments

One of the happiest moments in making a new book is to thank, as best as one can, those who helped create it. Even if there is only one author named on the cover, there are *always* many more who contributed to it.

When I used to travel to give lectures and workshops, Thea would always smile and say, as I was packing and heading for the airport, "Give beautiful lessons." This book is mostly "lessons" and I hope they are beautiful, because that is the heart of the matter. Thank you, Thea, for reminding me of this and for so much more.

I would also like to thank our daughters, Coleen and Alyda, for their unfailing support. Now there are also grandchildren who support these endeavors even when they don't realize it. Michael Macaluso, Alyda's husband, has also helped through quiet conversations during cookouts at the Macaluso home on their big deck looking out into the mountains.

Godly Play began as a family affair, so it is important that this last (or near last) book of mine about Godly Play will return to the family setting where it began. Over the decades many more people have been added to this "family." To my astonishment Godly Play now reaches far beyond Thea's and my original circle. The number of countries where Godly Play lives now is more than forty-three, but it keeps growing. Please go to www.GodlyPlayFoundation.org to find where in the world Godly Play is now. I wish I could visit all of you, Godlyplayers, but I send this book instead!

Among all those who helped with this book, I would like to especially mention Professor DeWitte Campbell Wyckoff (1918–2005). He helped give birth to Godly Play before anyone knew what it was or might become—including me. "Cam" was first my Christian education professor at Princeton Theological Seminary, then a mentor, and finally a friend. He made many significant contributions to Christian education theory and curriculum development and was working on *Theory and Design of Christian Education* when we met. He somehow found the time and a graceful way to help me discover my vocation, now almost sixty years ago. I am still in awe of the arrangement he made with the dean for me to have a tutorial with him rather than take the required Christian education course, which he taught and I found utterly frustrating.

Professor Wyckoff assigned me the task of writing my own theory of Christian education during the tutorial and I am still working on it. The paper I wrote for him was an earnest, typewritten piece full of spelling errors. The fundamental idea of teaching Christian language as a way to create existential meaning was just beginning to peek through the scattering of ideas. My experiences of God as a child pushed me in this direction and they still do. All I have written since my Princeton days is a commentary on that originating idea.

Cam was a wonderful listener. After I graduated he continued to help me think things through, as I continued to work on the theory he assigned me to write. I especially remember one day in his study at Princeton when he stood up, as we were talking, and went over to his wall of books. He pulled down a well-thumbed copy of one of Montessori's early books and handed it to me. "Have you read this?" I had, but this simple act exemplified Cam's mentoring. He supported my interest in Montessori by his quiet but serious acknowledgment of *his* interest. I never heard him mention Montessori before or after that sunny day, but his faith in me was clear.

The last time I saw Cam was in Albuquerque, where he and Mildred lived after his retirement. I was there for some meeting, which I have forgotten, but I will never forget having dinner with them at home. Cam was in his late seventies and this simple evening around the table with Mildred gave me the courage to carry on and still does.

Part of "carrying on" has usually involved finding a retreat for editing, thinking, and refreshment in an Italian restaurant wherever we lived. The place in South Denver has been Venice. I want to express my gratitude to everyone there for their help, but especially I want to mention Alessandro Carollo, Chef-Owner; Christian Delle Fave, Executive Chef; and Nunzio Marino, General Manager. As the years went by, Chris became my customary waiter at my customary table by the floor lamp, in the back corner. Last but not least I want to mention Leticca, who has always been very gracious often without speaking a word.

It has been a great pleasure to work again with Dirk deVries on this book. We have known each other for decades while he was director of the Denver-based education division of Church Publishing. He has published so many curricula that I have lost count, but this long list includes Godly Play. His help on this book came after his retirement from Church Publishing and brings his special talent as a photographer to the forefront. Those who have participated in his workshops on spirituality and photography can certainly testify to his art. He is the one who took the photographs for this book.

My new editor at Church Publishing is an old friend and someone who has been part of the world of Christian formation for decades. Sharon Pearson guided this book to its publication beautifully by her support, careful editing, creativity, and management. I would also like to thank Ryan Masteller, who produced this book, as he as done for most of my books at Church Publishing. It has always been a pleasure working with him and receiving his concise and perceptive comments to move things forward.

This is not a complete list of all those who helped, but to all of you, named and unnamed, I give thanks for making this book possible. I know there are still some errors in it of commission and omission, despite my best efforts, but they are mine and I gladly take responsibility for them all.

Jerome W. Berryman
June 4, 2017
Written with astonishment
on my 80th birthday

Introduction

This is a simple book, but it has taken a lifetime to write. The first six chapters are descriptions of how to present stories of God at home, told in a way that weaves them together with your family's stories. The seventh chapter is about reading classical children's books with your family and looking for the connections between them and this book's stories of God. The interplay between them helps interpret both. The last chapter reflects on how to meet family challenges by using Christian language to guide us into the deep channel of the creative process that flows out from and returns to God. We were born to be creators, so the deep current of the creative process is our true home. It is where families flourish.

When I say this book has taken "a lifetime to write," I mean that I have drawn on experiences of God from childhood to now. This includes my university, law school, and theological training as well as extensive experience in schools, hospitals, and churches, along with my postgraduate reading, writing, and teaching (which is also learning).

It is quite clear as I look back over eighty years, that the most important part of my learning has been sitting on the floor with circles of children for over forty years telling stories of God and wondering together with them about what the stories mean for our lives. In this book I have tried to apply what I discovered from the children in various settings about how to ground our families in God's overflowing creativity to meet the challenges we face.

Godly Play grew out of Thea's and my home, so I hope this book will nourish your families and the ideal of the Church as a family of families. May the ordinary church become a place of creative community beyond kinship, where the Creator and the creatures who create become one.

CHAPTER 1

The Story of God's Creating
The Creation

This book is about a long-term approach to celebrating your family and to prepare for unknown family challenges in the future. It shows how to do this in a deeply playful way by building up layers of family stories woven together with stories of God to fill a reservoir of meaning to draw from when needed.

We will begin by talking about how stories make meaning. We will then discuss the importance of being involved in nature to celebrate God's creation and to acknowledge our own true identity. We will then discuss what to do and say to weave together the celebration of creation with your own stories. We will close by discussing the remarkable ability of children to absorb God from nature and the implications of this for adults.

How Stories
Make Meaning

I came from a storytelling family, but I was in my mid-forties before I fully appreciated the value of that gift. I had to actually encounter families that didn't tell stories to discover just how important stories really are.

One of the most significant stories I heard as a child was a bedtime story about being a child in God's *creation*. This theme included God's creating, the creation as the product of God's creating, the presence of the Creator in God's creation, and our own creating that flows out of being created in God's image. None of this was made explicit at the time, but it was all there, waiting to be discovered in the decades that followed.

My dad sat on my bed in the soft light of evening and told me about playing outdoors when he was a little boy. I knew the places in my grandmother's yard where he had played, so in story and play we bridged three generations to be at home together in the richness of God's creation.

Our bond didn't have anything to do with talking specifically about God or religion, but the experience was very religious because it evoked places, where I, too, felt hints and whispers of God all around me as I played. Knowing God in God's creation was like what I later sensed when I found hints of the poet in the poem, the painter in the painting, the engineer in the machine, the physician in the healing, or the composer in the symphony. This is how I knew that the *experience* of God was present in my play and that my father and I shared this intuition. I could feel this. It was implied in his stories and his presence. The God-talk came later.

We adults sometimes forget how involved in nature we were as children, even in the city. This is why I would like to introduce you to Alister Hardy and the project he began after he retired as Linacre Professor of Zoology at Oxford. He had wondered all his life about the experiences of God he had felt as a child and wondered if others had also experienced such events. When he retired he invited people to send accounts of such experiences to The Religious Experience Research Unit (RERU), which he set up in 1969 at Manchester College, Oxford.[1]

Edward Robinson, a biologist, was the first director of RERU after Professor Hardy. He noticed that about 15 percent of the first 3,000 accounts they received referred to childhood experiences. He explored this surprising event in his book *The Original Vision* in 1977.

A Child's Experience of Nature and Its Implications for Adults

One of the beauties of Robinson's book is that he quoted at length from numerous accounts, rather than reducing them to tables of statistics. Important statistics are included in the book, but his quotations allow the reader to appreciate the texture and feeling of the writers' memories to make an informed interpretation of each story. I would like to quote from one of the RERU accounts so you can make up your own mind about the strengths and weaknesses of these memories.

Robinson acknowledged that our memories do not work like tape recorders. We interpret the past, as we remember it, looking back from new contexts in our later lives. This means that the *significance* of what happened counts as much as getting the details right. The account I would like to quote from involves horn-shaped lavender flowers on tall stalks appearing above "the gently swirling vapour" and a little girl's "black shoes with silver

---

1. This research is now located at the Alister Hardy Religious Experience Research Centre at the University of Wales Trinity Saint David in Lampeter, Wales.

buckles" that disappeared in the mist. The significance of this, however, was the point. The little girl pondered the meaning of this at the time of her experience and then re-worked that meaning for over fifty years.

> The most profound experience of my life came to me when I was very young—between four and five years old. I am not mistaken in dating this because I remember so clearly both the place where it occurred and the shoes I was wearing at the time, of which I was rather fond. Both of these facts relate only to this particular period in my life: I have a dated photograph of myself wearing the shoes in question.

> My mother and I were walking on a stretch of land in Pangbourne Berks, known locally as "the moors." As the sun declined and the slight chill of evening came on, a pearly mist formed over the ground. My feet, with the favourite black shoes with silver buckles, were gradually hidden from sight until I stood ankle deep in the gently swirling vapour. Here and there just the very tallest harebells appeared above the mist. I had a great love of these exquisitely formed flowers, and stood lost in wonder at the sight.

> Suddenly I seemed to see the mist as a shimmering gossamer tissue and the harebells, appearing here and there, seemed to shine with a brilliant fire. Somehow I understood that this was the living tissue of life itself, in which that which we call consciousness was embedded, appearing here and there as a shining focus of energy in the more diffused whole. In that moment I knew that I had my own special place, as had all other things, animate and so-called inanimate, and that we were all part of this universal tissue which was both fragile yet immensely strong, and utterly good and beneficent.

> The vision has never left me. It is as clear today as fifty years ago, and with it the same intense feeling of love of the world and the certainty of ultimate good. It gave me then a strong, clear sense of identity which has withstood many vicissitudes, and an affinity with plants, birds, animals, even insects, and people too, which has often been commented on. Moreover, the whole of this experience has ever since formed a kind of reservoir of strength fed from an unseen source, from which quite suddenly in the

midst of the very darkest times a bubble of pure joy rises through it all, and I know that whatever the anguish there is some deep centre in my life which cannot be touched by it.

Of course, at the early age of four or five I could not have expressed anything of the experience in the words I have now used, and perhaps the attempt to convey the absorption of myself into the whole, and the intensity of meaning, sounds merely over-coloured to the reader. But the point is that, by whatever mysterious perception, the whole impression and its total meaning were apprehended in a single instant. Years later, reading Traherne and Meister Eckhart and Francis of Assisi, I have cried aloud with surprise and joy, knowing myself to be in the company of others, who had shared the same kind of experience and who had been able to set it down so marvelously. This is not the only experience of the kind that has come to me—indeed they occur relatively often—but it is without doubt the one which has laid the deepest foundations of my life, and for which I feel the profoundest gratitude.[2]

This story is remarkable for many reasons, but I would like to draw your attention to only one aspect of it. The little girl's original vision was not forgotten. It continued to give her life meaning as an adult. She was not only the speaker of her memory. She was also the listener. She listened long and well to her memory over the years and continued to interpret it, giving her life renewed meaning.

When children try to tell us about a numinous experience, like the one on the moors, they risk having their treasured discoveries causally dismissed by adults. If children object to this trivialization by adults and stand up for the reality they have experienced, they risk being put down again or, even worse, being punished or shunned for advocating for it. This teaches children to mistrust adults' interpretations about such experiences *and* their own childhood experience of them. The result is a double bind that blocks children's spirituality. Their experience of God risks being demeaned if they speak up and they demean their own experience if they don't.

2. Edward Robinson, *The Original Vision* (Lampeter, Wales: Religious Experience Research Unit, 1977), 34.

Sometimes children are strong enough to retain a significant memory, like "the living tissue of life itself," which grounds them in the deepest, most creative, part of their identity. They know they are part of God's creation, which gives them a "reservoir of strength fed from an unseen source." As children grow older they begin to realize, like the little girl on the moors did, that others have experienced something like they did and that they "had been able to set it down so marvelously." It is my great hope that this approach to stories of God at home will avoid the double bind and help nourish these treasured memories from childhood so they can develop fully across the decades.

Edward Robinson's study quoted many memories of children who had resisted the double bind and retained their early memories into adulthood. One adult, remembering himself as a little boy, wrote, "This inner knowledge was exciting and absorbingly interesting, but it remained unsaid because, even if I could have expressed it, no one would have understood. Once, when I tried, I was told I was morbid."[3] He was able to retain this significant memory, because, as he said, "I knew what I knew." I hope this sort of confidence in the significance of one's early experience of God will be strengthened by this approach to family storytelling and listening, so our early experiences of God can enrich and renew each decade of our lives.

One wonders how many of the 85 percent of the respondents, who did not mention childhood experiences, had lost access to their stories of God because of the double bind. The family celebrations in this book are designed to support free access to our early experiences of God and to provide the language for their memories to be enriched. The telling and interpreting of such stories, as we said, is a potent source of meaning to sustain family flourishing.

In 1997 Kevin M. Bradt, S.J. published *Story as a Way of Knowing*. He gathered up many of the themes in the air at the time and gave them his own creative shape as a Jesuit psychotherapist and teacher at the Jesuit School of Theology in Berkeley, California. Bradt wanted to emphasize how narrative meaning is the co-creation of the teller and the hearer, so he

---

3. Robinson, 13.

called this relational knowing "storying" to avoid the undue emphasis on the telling of stories by such terms as "storyteller" or "storytelling." This is why our goal here is to show how "to story" the Creation.

"Storying" the Creation

"Storying" God's creation involves the *Creator*, the *creating itself, what is created*, how the creation *points to* its Creator and how God's image is the creative process within us. The point of mentioning this complexity again is to say that when we "story" the creation, we need to be aware that the richness of this experience overflows the narrative, even when aspects of it are not mentioned.

We begin with a box full of materials. They help communicate the many levels and perspectives of creation. These materials also insure that the richness of the narrative is open to all the stages and ages of those gathered. You can literally grasp the story with your hands and other senses to help grasp it with your mind and spirit.

You might keep this box with your camping gear, if that is something your family does, or somewhere in the home where you keep treasured things. Where you put the box of materials matters. It makes a statement of value about this story of God *and* your family. The box has a yellow circle on it. This represents the original light, which God gave us on the first day of creation. The first six chapters begin with an image of such a box and its contents. They also include a picture of the material as it is presented.

In this presentation and the ones that follow, much will be said about "the family." What I mean by "the family" includes your immediate family but also those that your family has adopted as unofficial members. When you invite "the family" to gather for these presentations, you might include friends, older and younger, who share a special relationship with you.

Inside the box are seven, small wooden plaques and a piece of black cloth that begins all rolled up. The black felt is the "underlay," which is rolled out on the family table or outside on the ground if that is where the story is told and heard. Unroll it from your right to left and lay the plaques on the felt in the same way so they can be "read" from left to right by those gathered

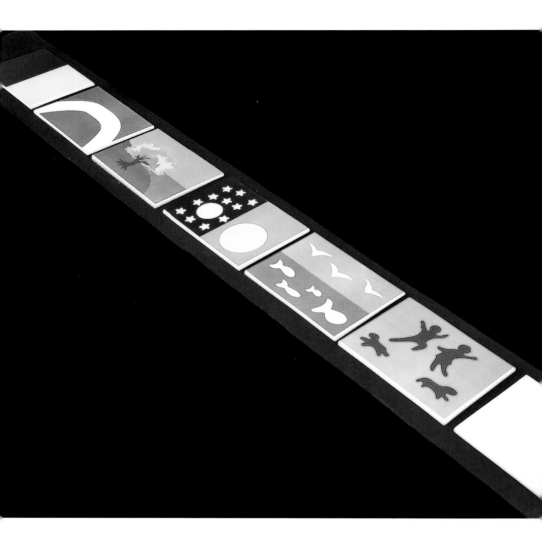

to watch, listen, and wonder. This material, like the others described in this book, is available from Godly Play Resources, which is part of the nonprofit, Godly Play Foundation. You can learn more about training and resources from the website www.godlyplayfoundation.org.

The rectangular pieces of wood represent light, water, dry land, day and night, the creatures that fly and swim, the creatures that walk upon the earth, and finally a day to rest and reflect on all the gifts of creation. This material is a smaller version of the Godly Play presentation, "The Creation," which has been adapted for the home and for use outside in nature.[4] If your children are in a Godly Play program, the materials described in this book will be familiar but not too familiar, since they are smaller and the presentations are woven together with family stories.

We will talk more about the leader as this book develops, but for now it is enough to say that the leader needs to be informal and relaxed to invite wonder and yet be clearly in charge so the experience is a safe place where thoughts can be freely expressed. A rich sense of humor helps make this possible.

The leader participates in the story, but also supports the responses at the end of the presentation about the family's experiences of nature and their meaning. Some family members need to be coaxed a little to take part while others need to be toned down so they don't dominate the wondering. When the energy begins to decline in the wondering, the leader closes "the storying" while everyone is still interested. Everything is put back in the box and the "Amen" is said.

Let's now take a look at the specific actions and words that make up the telling and hearing of this story of God. It is always good to remember that *what is done* and *how it is done* are as important as *what is said*. This is why the "movements" are placed first in the script at the left.

What to Do and What to Say

MOVEMENTS

WORDS

Pick up the box. Look at it with appreciation and curiosity, then place it ceremonously back on the table (or on the earth if you are outside). Look at those gathered and speak quietly but with energy and focus.

Today we remember where we came from, so let's go all the way back to the beginning and a little before the beginning.

4. Jerome W. Berryman, *The Complete Guide to Godly Play, Volume 2: Revised and Expanded* (New York: Church Publishing, 2017), 41–48.

Move the box to one side and remove the lid. Put the box inside the lid. Take out the rolled-up underlay and place it in front of you. Look at it with curiosity and respect, then slowly unroll it all the way from right to left as you say:

In the beginning there was . . . well, there wasn't very much, except, perhaps, an enormous smile.

Trace the "enormous smile" from one end of the underlay to the other. Make the smile so it faces the others.

Take the first plaque from the box, Hold it for a moment with two hands, showing it to the others as you say:

Then on the very first day God gave us the gift of light.

This was not ordinary light. It was the light that all the rest of the light comes from.

Place the plaque to your right on the underlay. After laying the plaque on the underlay, place your hand on it gently but firmly like a blessing and say:

When God saw the light God said, "It is good," and that was the end of the first day.

Take out the second plaque and hold it with two hands as you say:

On the second day God gave us the gift of water.

This was not ordinary water. It was the water that all the rest of the water comes from.

Place the plaque on the underlay to your left of the first one. After laying the plaque on the underlay, place your hand on it gently but firmly like a blessing and say:

When God saw the water God said, "It is good," and that was the end of the second day.

There is an arch of white on this card to represent "the firmament," so be sure that the plaque is turned so that it looks like an arch to those watching. Don't say anything about "the firmament" at this time. Wait until someone asks about it, or on another day you might say, "I wonder what this could be."

Take out the third plaque, hold it with two hands, showing it to the others as you say:

On the third day God gave us the gift of the dry land and the green and growing things.

Place the plaque on the underlay. Put your hand on it like a blessing as you say:

When God saw the dry land and the green and growing things God said, "It is good," and that was the end of the third day.

Take out the fourth plaque, hold it for a moment, showing it to the others, then place it on the underlay to the left of the dry land as you say:

On the fourth day God gave us the gift of the day and the night so we can count our days. God gave us time.

Place the plaque on the underlay, then place your hand on it like a blessing.

When God saw the day and the night, God said, "It is good," and that was the end of the fourth day.

Take out the next plaque and show it to the others as you say:

On the fifth day God gave us the gift of all the creatures that swim and all the creatures that fly.

Place the plaque and then put your hand on it like a blessing.

When God saw all the creatures that swim and all the creatures that fly, God said, "It is good," and that was the end of the fifth day.

Take out the next plaque from the box, hold it with two hands, showing it to the others, and say:

On the sixth day God gave us the gift of the creatures that walk upon the earth, the creatures that walk with two legs like you and like I and those that walk with many legs. And God placed the Image of God, the Creator, within us.

Place the plaque on the underlay and then put your hand on it like a blessing as you say:

When God saw all the creatures that walk upon the earth and the great gifts of all the other days, God said, "It is very good," and that was the end of the sixth day.

*Take out the last plaque, showing
it to the others as you say:*

On the seventh day, God rested and gave us a day to rest and remember the great gifts of all the other days.

*Place the plaque on the underlay,
then say:*

There is nothing on this plaque because I don't know where you like to go to rest and remember the great gifts. I wonder what place is best for you to do this?[5]

---

5. Wondering "questions" (or perhaps "wonderings") end with a question mark. They are not quite a statement or a question but something else. They acknowledge our mutual standing before the mystery of God with amazement. They deserve their own unique punctuation mark, but we don't have one.

A question entails an answer by the way it is posed, but a wondering is about something you don't know the answer to. If you know the answer to a wondering, then it is not a wondering.

An example of what I mean by a question entailing its answer is, "What time is it?" You know there is an answer to this and that it can be stated. Sometimes questions go so far as to imply a specific proposition by the way they are asked. A famous example is, "Have you stopped beating your wife?" The beating is implied in the question. There are also Socratic questions. This is when a teacher, like Socrates, asks questions that lead students to arrive at the answer the teacher already has in mind.

Wonderings invite those listening to join together to honor each unique, personal response to God's mystery. For example there are four classic wonderings about sacred stories in Godly Play. I wonder what part of this story you like best? I wonder what part is the most important part? I wonder where you are in the story? I wonder what part of the story we can leave out and still have all the story we need? All four of these wonderings respect the experience of others and the mystery of God's presence. Wondering invites us to join together in our wondering even though we will likely arrive at different responses.

After the conversation winds down, sit back and look at all of the days of creation. Open both hands and extend them to show the wholeness of all the days. Pause and take a deep breath. Reach out and touch the first plaque again.

Now, I wonder if anyone in this family noticed the light this morning when you opened your eyes? I wonder what it was like? I wonder what your favorite kind of light might be?

Participate in but still guide the wondering. Be sure that all those who wish to speak have a chance. When the conversation loses its energy, place your hand on the second plaque.

I wonder if you touched or tasted water today? What did it feel like? What was its taste? I wonder what the scariest water was, you ever saw? What was the most peaceful? I wonder what makes water beautiful?

Place your hand on the third plaque.

Did you know that every time you put your foot down, you place it on holy ground? God gave us this gift. I wonder how we can say "Thank you"?

Encourage those to speak who don't know what to say. Share your thoughts, but be careful not to stop the wondering by your comments. Some may think you have all the right answers. When the wondering begins to lose its energy, place your hand on the fourth plaque.

I wonder how time feels as it passes by? I wonder what the best way is for you to keep time? I wonder how old our family really is? I wonder how old time is?

Participate in the wondering, but still guide it so all can speak who wish to. When the conversation loses its energy, touch the fifth plaque.

I wonder what it's like to fly on invisible air? I wonder if water is invisible to fish? I wonder why God made so many kinds of birds and fish? I wonder where all these creatures are going?

Participate in the conversation unless you feel that you are intruding and blocking it. Be sure that all who want to talk have a chance to speak. When the conversation begins to lose its momentum, place your hand on the sixth plaque.

I wonder how people are different from the other animals? I wonder if you can feel God's image inside of you? I wonder where the Creator's creativity came from? I wonder if you have ever seen creating taking place?

Take part in the conversation, but be sure that everyone who wishes to speak has an opportunity. When the conversation loses its energy, place your hand on the seventh plaque.

I wonder why God made this day? I wonder what its gift really is? I wonder how resting and remembering helps? I wonder why there is something instead of nothing?

Pause and reflect silently on the whole series of plaques, touching each one. You then begin to pick up each one, naming it as you put it back into the box. Roll up the underlay and put it away. As you do this, say:

Our family is part of this story. Thanks be to God!

Replace the lid with ceremony.

Amen.

The "Amen" brings the presentation to a close.

You have now experienced what it is like to tell a story of God and invite your family to take part in it. We will have more to say about telling and hearing stories in the next chapter. To close this chapter let's talk just a bit more about children and adults experiencing the Creator in nature, since that is what this story of God is about.

Experiencing the Creator in Nature for All Ages

Children and adults experience God in three major ways. God comes to us from *beyond* as the Creator. God also comes from *beside us* as Jesus, whom we read about in the Gospels and know by experience, as the apostle Paul did on the road to Damascus in the first century. God also comes from beside us by shining through our fellow creatures. The third way God comes to us is from *within* as the Holy Spirit. We know God in these three ways all the time, no matter where we are or whether we are paying attention or not. The Holy Trinity is always with us informing us who we truly are.

There is a broad developmental map for knowing the Holy Trinity. Children are especially good at knowing God as the Creator through their absorbing of God's presence in nature. Adolescents and young adults often prefer reading about and debating the meaning of Jesus' life and death. Middle and older adults tend to know God from within, because it often takes a long time for the rich awareness of one's deep identity as a creator in God's image to become conscious in an integrated way. Still, these developmental tendencies do not always hold. All ages and types of people can know God in any or all of these three ways at any time, because the only limit to God is that God is unlimited.

Let's focus now on the remarkable ability of children to absorb God through God's creation and the implications of this intuitive sensitivity for adults. Our guide will be Richard N. Coe's 1984 study of autobiographies about childhood called *When the Grass Was Taller.* Coe read some 600 autobiographies in many languages that involved childhood, and established this genre of literature formally, which he called "Childhoods." A more recent study in this area is John Pridmore's *Playing with Icons*, published by The Center for the Theology of Childhood in 2017. The Center is part of the nonprofit Godly Play Foundation.

Coe argued that children's knowing cannot be "conveyed by the utilitarian logic of the responsible adult," because childhood "constitutes an alternative dimension" out of which the wholeness of an "inner, symbolic truth" is lived. The world speaks first to the child as a whole and the child responds, not the other way around. We adults put our specific questions to nature and work out our answers by the scientific method. Children absorb nature, including hints of God, in an undifferentiated way through their senses and contemplative abilities. They know God by intuition, as part of this unitive knowing.

Coe noticed three things about the world of childhood from his reading of the remembered childhood experiences.[6] All three discoveries were difficult to put into language, but Coe tried anyway. He said that the world of children is an "alternative experience," a kind of "magic," and a sense of "abundance."

The "alternative experience" he noticed is an alternative to the world known by adults. It is a world of play in the deepest sense with its own logic, rituals, and sensualities. Coe argued that being able to enter this world is what gives the writer the ability to recreate childhood and the motive for attempting it. He went further to say that being able to re-enter this experience as adults is the source for all poetry.

Second, children experience "magic" in the world around them. Coe tried to protect the word "magic" from trivialization, because he could not find a better word to convey what he meant. He did not mean "mere nostalgia for a carefree past, a lost innocence." What he *did* mean was an "exaltation beyond language—yet for which, since it is an experience so momentous, eventually a language must be found." In the alternative world of childhood, there is a different way of being from the everyday adult world. Childhood involves "mystic exaltation," like that of the little girl on the moors, mentioned in Robinson's *The Original Vision*.

Third, there is a sense of "abundance." Coe did not mean merely material abundance in the sense of "a well-stocked larder." The abundance of childhood seems to be independent of what money can buy, which he noticed from his reading of memories from disadvantaged homes. Childhood involves a kind of abundance that is "a universe which is full; of being crowded in on all sides by sounds and colors, by flowers, butterflies and

---

6. Richard N. Coe, *When the Grass Was Taller: Autobiography and the Experience of Childhood* (New Haven, CT: Yale University Press, 1984), 285–87.

grasses, by streetlamps and fireworks and transfers[7] and sweets with marvelous names in many-colored wrappers."[8] Coe suggested that one of the reasons that Christmas celebrations appeal to children and adults is their sense of abundance. A truly unhappy Christmas is not one in which children receive no toys but one that is emotionally empty and the child is isolated. Such a Christmas expresses spiritual emptiness rather than abundance.

The experience of God from beyond is a natural part of the child's world. We will continue to explore how God comes to us in all three ways as the book continues, but for now let's sum up "storying" God's creation and link this chapter to the next one, where we will continue layering stories of God and weaving them together with family stories to create a reservoir of meaning to draw from when needed for family challenges.

Conclusion

This chapter focused on the story of God, the Creator, and how family stories can be woven together with it. The emphasis was on how to do this and why. The story of God's creating is a good one to begin with, because it can be presented anytime and anywhere, indoors or outdoors. Most of the stories to follow are tied to specific times of the year.

The story of God creating is also about how the creative process was given to our forbearers at the beginning of everything and to each one of us at our birth. The Hebrew sages sensed this and expressed it beautifully at the beginning of Genesis.

As we continue to reflect on " storying," you will probably notice that the language used in these presentations is as open to children as it is to adults. The materials, your movements, the sound of your voice, and your ease at being a natural storyteller combine with the breadth and depth of the

---

7. Richard Coe is an Australian, so I wrote to Judyth Roberts, a leader in the Australian College of Godly Play Trainers, on April 7, 2017, to see what Coe was referring to by the term "transfers." A transfer is a picture that was fixed onto "a sort of cellophane that when wiped with a damp clothe and pressed would transfer the picture onto another surface." Judyth also wrote that transfers were very popular in Australia from the 1930s to about 1950. Her mother talked about collecting and playing with them as a child.

8. Coe, 287.

words to invite old and young to respond honestly and openly. This is one of the reasons why this approach works well in families involving three or more generations and where English is not the first language for everyone.

You also may have noticed that when I write "Church," I mean the ideal church we all aspire to. When I write "church," which is most of the time, the reference is to the ordinary, flawed institution we all experience and which we seek to help move closer to the ideal with God's grace.

In the next chapter we will translate the church's celebration of Christmas into a story of God for the home. We will look at Christmas next because it is the church celebration most likely to be attended by families, but we also need to understand that there is a logic that ties Creation, Christmas, Easter, and Pentecost together, whether celebrated in the home or in a church setting. This is why after Christmas we will "story" Easter and then Pentecost.

After the Creation, Christmas, Easter, and Pentecost chapters, we will present the Good Shepherd in chapter 5, which is about the nature of God and how we participate in it. Chapter 6 will "story" a synthesis of the first five chapters by using the liturgical circle of the church year. We will then discuss stories *about the stories* of God and conclude by saying more directly how the whole book helps us prepare for and cope with family challenges.

CHAPTER 2

The Story of God with Us
Christmas

21

Stories are like the air we breathe. They are invisible and taken for granted until they are missing, then we quickly discover we can't live without them. This is because stories tell who we are and they unite us. This is why it is almost impossible to meet family challenges without them. Let's begin, then, with a story about the importance of stories.

A Story about the Importance of Stories

I worked at Houston Child Guidance Center from 1983 to 1985 as part of an interdisciplinary team that cared for suicidal children and their families. The team included a psychiatrist, a psychologist, a social worker, an M.D. drug expert, and myself, an Episcopal priest. We provided family systems therapy and studied what had gone wrong in the relationships that resulted in children trying to kill themselves.

What these families had in common was that they did not tell stories. They did not tell stories about vacations, funny things that happened, sad things, grandparents, births, deaths, pets, hopes, trips, dreams, or any other tales I took for granted, since I had come from a storytelling family. Their communication was reduced to commands, demands, exclamations, brief explanations, and questions requiring short, factual answers. The family members were like neighboring islands without any bridges. There was no narrative to connect them. What was the treatment? We set up ways to encourage them to tell stories face-to-face.

This discovery caused me to move from teaching medical ethics in the Texas Medical Center from 1974 to1984, where Godly Play was used in the hospitals, to Christ Church Cathedral in downtown Houston to tell stories. I wanted to help families tell their stories and find their place in the Great Story. I had learned firsthand that human beings cannot live without significant stories, so I intended to contribute to families in what ways I could, as someone who knew how and why "to story." The experience at the Cathedral from 1984 to 1994 contributed to the continuing development of Godly Play in the congregational setting and in schools.

The uniqueness of spoken narrative, as way of knowing, is easy to overlook. We have become so accustomed to living in the print world of reading and writing that we have learned without fully realizing it to value texts (and texting) more than talking face-to-face.

The difference between texts and talk is dramatic. With texts, the words are present but the people are absent. With speaking, the people are present but the words disappear as soon as they are spoken except for memories, which can differ.

Spoken narrative supported by gestures was one of the earliest ways our forbearers made meaning. This kind of communication formed and was formed by the evolution of our brains across vast eras of time. Our ancestors appeared in Africa some 200,000 years ago, but the first texts did not appear until about 3500–3000 BCE in ancient Sumer and Akkad in what today is southern Iraq. Our ancestors pushed wedge-shaped reeds into wet clay and then baked the text to preserve it. These ancient texts are still being discovered today and involve several different writing systems, but the important thing about them all is that they were relatively permanent. Today you can visit the British Museum and still find some 130,000 clay tablets that can be read from left to right in neat lines that cover all aspects of ancient life from bills of sale to religious texts and love songs.

Storytelling and story listening continued to survive alongside ancient texts, but today something new has been added. When we make oral-auditory meaning with someone, the person we are talking to might be electronically "texting" an invisible reader while we are talking to them face-to-face.

As we discussed in the last chapter, the meaning made by "storying" is found in the connections between the people involved. It is impossible for isolated, context-less meaning to be *spoken*, because the context is involved in the meaning made. This is why merely showing up for oral-auditory communication is not enough. It requires active and reflective listening *to hear* the meaning made and to discover why it matters. This is how spoken stories hold families together and why it is so important "to story" Christmas at home face-to-face.

"Storying" Christmas

Christmas is about children. It celebrates you as a child, your children, (biological, adopted, or befriended)[1] grandchildren (biological, adopted, or befriended), and God's child. Christmas evokes the wonder of children and our wonder about them. The mystery of the Incarnation, when considered deeply in all its implications, needs to be encountered with wonder to open the movement of the creative process in us. This movement makes us part of the birth that Christmas celebrates. Fortunately, we don't need to begin our thinking about Christmas with the Incarnation. Children are wonderful enough to contemplate and each one implies the Incarnation, because all children are all born with the image of the Creator within them.

Christmas is a time to wonder and to wonder about wonder, but wonder is not aggressive. It does not fight for its own space in the heightened busyness and business of the season. It can be scheduled out with ease, because it is unscheduled by nature. Wonder marks the moment when the unexpected invades the expected, such as when our normal world is disrupted by sublime beauty or awful tragedy. This means that we need to give wonder a chance to be experienced during Christmas so it can ripen and produce a richness of Christmas never before realized.

If we are not expectant and open to Christmas, we can walk right through its mystery and not even know it's there. Miracles are all around us, but if we don't take time to notice or fully appreciate them, they go unnoticed, which impoverishes us. Christmas, which is the miracle of miracles, is no different than any other miracle in this regard, so "storying" God's birth is well worth it.

To story God's birth at home we will use words and story-making materials like those used in Godly Play. They are smaller and slightly different from the longer Godly Play versions, which are used in churches, schools, and elsewhere.[2] The home version of Godly Play also has a different purpose. It is to help integrate the stories of your family with the stories of God.

---

1. My definition of "family" includes those who are adopted and befriended as well as genetically kin. All three groups are "natural" as part of the family.

2. Jerome W. Berryman, *The Complete Guide To Godly Play, Volume 3: Revised and Expanded* (New York: Church Publishing, 2017), 25–59.

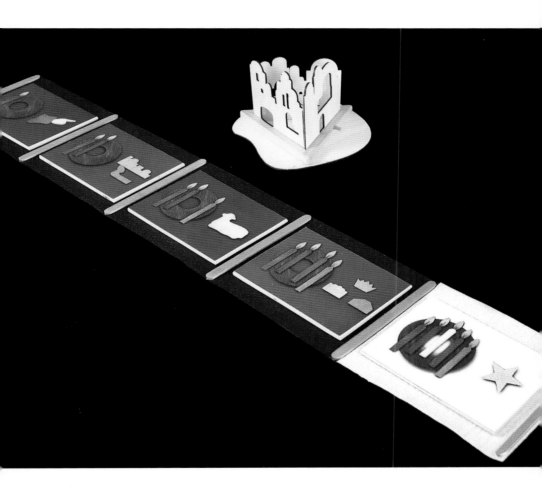

The presentation pieces are kept in a wooden box with a star on top, because like the *magi*, we too, are following the star to find the birth of a rumored mystery in this celebration. This is why you will find inside the box a symbolic model of Bethlehem, the destination for our imagination. There is also a strip of felt, like a pathway, which we will call an "underlay." It has four purple or blue panels with one white one at the end. These panels represent the four Sundays of Advent and Christmas Day, which may not be on a Sunday. The underlay is rolled up so Christmas is "inside" Advent, like a seed is inside its pod. You will place a plaque on each of the appropriate panels, as the narrative is unrolled.

You can make this material yourself or order it already made, like in the picture. These materials are made by Godly Play Resources, which is part of the nonprofit Godly Play Foundation. These materials can be found at www.godlyplayresources.com. The Foundation supports the practice of Godly Play around the world.

You might keep these materials with your other Christmas things, and a family discussion about where to keep the box is a good idea. It is important that the material be beautiful and well cared for to show the value you give to the mystery of Christmas and the wonder of your family. There is a deep connection between religion, beauty, family, and wonder.

In addition to the beautiful materials, you need a leader to guide the telling and hearing of the story. The leader helps everyone relax and participate in what takes place. The leader needs to be a calm, non-anxious presence but still firmly in charge. If you have a good leader and a beautiful material "to story" Christmas at home, the making of meaning will take care of itself. All you have to do is follow the script and be open to the wondering. We will come to the script in a moment, but first, let's say just a bit more about the leader.

In some Christian traditions the liturgical leader is called "the celebrant." The celebrant presides at the altar, which is often called the communion "table." Using your family table to tell and hear the story points to the celebration at the table in the church. Your family table is an important place, even if you don't gather there much for meals and conversation. It is ideally a symbol of sustenance and creative unity, so it is usually a good place to nurture your family's circle of meaning and the creative process that keeps it alive. We will have more to say about the creative process as the book continues.

Human beings all over the world use rituals to create order, community, and meaning for their lives. Rituals have been given a bad name by associating them with compulsive acts done for unconscious reasons, like "ritual" hand washing. There is no danger of that here. The "storying" rituals in this book stimulate too much creativity, play, love, and spirituality for this to happen.

All the leader does is pick up the box and set it down again to begin. The leader might stand up to do this or remain seated. Standing may seem a little pretentious, but some people can do this without getting so formal that formality gets in the way.

Move the box to one side without hurrying after it is reset on the table. The lid is then removed and the things inside the box are taken out. A few words are said as the story develops and the family responds. Even if no one responds, the process will still take care of itself. All you have to do is *actually begin*. The ritual's naturalness and ease will mature gracefully as those around the table become accustomed to weaving their stories together with the stories of God.

The leader ends the celebration, as the conversation winds down, by saying "Amen" (So be it.) and putting everything back in the box. This pattern will be used for all the stories of God. The things in the box support this pattern. They are symbolic to help probe what is essential in the story, but let's not make too much out of that. They are also the "pieces" used to play this game to make ultimate meaning, but let's not get distracted by that either. Instead, let's just continue describing generally how the "storying" of Christmas works at your family table.

The first thing you, as the leader, take out of the box is the rolled-up piece of felt with five panels. It is unrolled from your right to left, so those gathered can "read" what's placed on it from left to right, the way we are accustomed to reading written narratives. The plaques are placed on the panels facing those gathered around the table.

As each new Sunday in Advent arrives, the previous plaques are placed on the underlay and briefly mentioned to build up the story for the image of the day. On Christmas Day all four images of Advent are again laid out to recall your preparation and then the plaque for the great mystery of God's Nativity[3] is placed on the underlay for the family to experience.

There is nothing really new about this sort of preparation. The word "Advent" itself has always encouraged expectant waiting. It is an old, venerable word, which comes from the Latin *adventus*, which means approaching and arrival. Both experiences are present in this story of God.

---

3. To expand on the idea of "Nativity," please see the fable "Steady (Not Stable) Nativity" in Jerome W. Berryman, *Becoming Like a Child: The Curiosity of Maturity beyond the Norm* (New York: Church Publishing, 2017), 181–87.

With this introduction we are now ready to present what to do and what to say. The action is written on the left because it sets the context and spirit for speaking and hearing the words. What you say is on the right of the script, because the words are also important. The words are conceived to be open to all ages and kinds of people, but they need to be said with love, because Christian language is the language of love.

The script assumes that you will use the royal color purple to help prepare for Christmas, but many churches use Mary's color, which is blue. If you would like to use blue for your underlay, please let the people at Godly Play Resources know when you order your materials. They already understand this and are ready to help you. Now, let's see more specifically what "storying" Christmas involves.

What to Do and What to Say

The First Sunday in Advent

MOVEMENTS	WORDS
Pick up the box and look at it with curiosity and respect. Place it ceremoniously back on the table. Look at those gathered and say quietly but with intensity:	This is the time when we get ready to come close to the mystery of Christmas. It is the time we call "Advent."
Move the box to one side and remove the lid. Put the box inside the lid. Take out the model of Bethlehem and put it together. Place it on the table between you and the others.	Here is Bethlehem. This is the season when we are *all* on our way to Bethlehem.

Take out the underlay and place it on the table to your right between you and the model of Bethlehem.

This is also the time of the color purple, the color of kings and queens. It is a serious and sometimes sad color. It shows that a king is coming to Bethlehem, but *this* king was not the kind of king anyone thought was coming.

Unroll the underlay to your left to show the first panel.

Place the first plaque on the underlay.

Today is the first Sunday in Advent.

Point to Bethlehem as you speak.

This is the time when we remember the prophets and how they pointed the way. Prophets know what is important, even when others don't. They knew that something wonderful was going to happen in Bethlehem that would change everything.

You then pause, and, taking plenty of time, touch the first plaque.

Now, I wonder if there is anyone in this family who has ever known a prophet?

Look questioningly at those who are gathered at the table. Invite them to speak, using your manner as much as your words.

Each year the wondering will seem more natural. Besides, just because people don't say anything doesn't mean that they aren't wondering to themselves silently.

Be sure to be supportive and be sure that everyone who wants to has a chance to speak. When the wondering is finished, the leader concludes by saying:

Our family is part of this story. Thanks be to God!

Put everything back into the box without hurrying. When everything is returned, replace the lid and say:

Amen.

Conversation might continue as people leave the table.

The Second Sunday in Advent

Pick up the box, look at it with curiosity and respect. Place it ceremoniously back on the table.

Look at the people and say:

This is the time when we get ready to come close to the mystery of Christmas. It is the time we call "Advent."

Move the box to one side and remove the lid. Put the box inside the lid. Take out the model of Bethlehem and put it together. Place it on the table between you and the others.

Here is Bethlehem. This is the season when we are *all* on our way to Bethlehem.

Take out the underlay. Place it on the table to your right between you and the model of Bethlehem.

This is the time of the color purple, the color of kings and queens. It is a serious and sometimes sad color. It shows that a king is coming to Bethlehem, but *this* king was not the kind of king anyone thought was coming.

Unroll the first panel.

On the first Sunday in Advent, we remembered the prophets.

Place the first plaque on the underlay.

Unroll the second panel. Hold the second plaque in your hands and show it to the others.

Today we remember how the mother Mary and the father Joseph made their way to Bethlehem.

Place the second plaque on the under-lay. Contemplate it for a moment, perhaps tracing the figures with your finger.

Now, I wonder if there is anyone in this family who ever went on a great journey?

Look at those who are gathered around at the table. Invite them to speak, using your manner as much as your words.

Just because people don't say things out loud, does not mean that they aren't wondering silently within.

Be supportive and be sure that everyone who wants to speak has a chance. When the wondering is finished, you conclude by saying:

Our family is part of this story. Thanks be to God!

Put everything back in the box without hurrying. When everything is put back, the lid is replaced and the celebration is complete. Say:

Amen.

Conversation might continue as people leave the table.

The Third Sunday in Advent

Pick up the box and look at it with care and curiosity. Put it back ceremoniously on the table. Look at the people gathered and say:

This is the time when we get ready to come close to the mystery of Christmas. It is the time we call "Advent."

Move the box to one side, remove the lid, and put the box inside the lid. Take out the model of Bethlehem and put it together. Place it on the table between you and the others.

Here is Bethlehem. This is the season when we are *all* on our way to Bethlehem.

Take out the underlay and place it on the table to your right between you and the model of Bethlehem.

This is the time of the color purple, the color of kings and queens. It is a serious and sometimes sad color. It shows that a king is coming to Bethlehem, but *this* king was not the kind of king anyone thought was coming.

Unroll the panels as needed.

The first Sunday in Advent, we remembered the prophets.

Place the first plaque on the underlay.

The second Sunday in Advent, we remembered how the mother Mary and the father Joseph made their way to Bethlehem.

Place the second plaque on the underlay.

Pick up the third plaque and show it to the others.

Today we remember the shepherds in the fields, keeping their flocks by night. They heard singing in the sky and saw a great light, so they ran to see the little king.

Place it on the underlay. Consider it for a moment, perhaps tracing the figures for a moment, and then say:

Now, I wonder if there is anyone in this family who has ever heard or seen mysterious things?

*Look at those gathered at the table.
Invite them to speak by using your
manner as much as your words.*

*Be sure to be supportive and help
everyone who wants to speak have
a chance. When the wondering is
finished, conclude by saying:*

**Our family is part of this story.
Thanks be to God!**

*Put everything back in the box without
hurrying. When everything is put back,
replace the lid and the celebration is
complete. Say:*

Amen.

*Conversation might continue as
people leave the table.*

The Fourth Sunday in Advent

*Pick up the box and look at it with
curiosity and respect. Place it
ceremoniously back on the table.
Look at the people gathered and
say:*

**This is the time when we get ready
to come close to the mystery of
Christmas. It is the time we call
"Advent."**

Move the box to one side and remove the lid. Place the box in the lid. Take out the model of Bethlehem and put it together. Place it on the table between you and the others.

Here is Bethlehem. This is the season when we are *all* on our way to Bethlehem.

Take out the underlay. Place it on the table to your right between you and Bethlehem.

This is the time of the color purple, the color of kings and queens. It is a serious and sometimes sad color. It shows that a king is coming to Bethlehem, but *this* king was not the kind of king anyone thought was coming.

Unroll the panels, as needed.

On the first Sunday in Advent, we remembered the prophets.

Place the first plaque.

On the second Sunday in Advent, we remembered how the mother Mary and father Joseph made their way to Bethlehem.

Place the second plaque.

On the third Sunday in Advent, we remembered the shepherds in the fields keeping their flocks by night. They heard singing in the sky and saw a great light, so they ran to see the little king.

Place the third plaque.

Today we remember how the three kings, the "wise men," the *magi*, followed the star to find the baby, to adore[4] him, and to give him gifts.

Place the fourth plaque on the underlay. Contemplate it for a moment, perhaps tracing the figures with your finger.

Now, I wonder if anyone in this family has ever adored a child or given gifts?

Look at those who are gathered at the table. Invite them to speak, using more your manner than urging them by your words.

---

4. We don't use the verb "to adore" much these days. We might say "adorable," as an adjective, but the meaning stressed here is an action that is more than something sweet and charming although that is part of it. "To adore" the Christ child is complex, which Thomas Aquinas (1225–1274) suggested in one of his five beautiful hymns, written to honor the gift of Christ's presence in the Blessed Sacrament at the request of Pope Urban IV. It begins:

Adoro te devote, latens Deitas,	I devoutly adore you, O hidden deity
Quae sub his figuris vere latitas;	Truly hidden beneath these appearances
Tibi se cor meum totum subjicit	My whole heart submits to you,
Quia te contemplans totum deficit.	And in contemplating you, it surrenders itself completely.

The adoration of the Christ Child involves God being hidden beneath "appearances." Thomas's poetry about the bread and wine of the Mass suggests how God is always hidden and revealed at the same time. This is also true for the Christ Child in Christmas and God in all of God's creation.

The *magi* gave gifts to the Christ Child in addition to adoring him. Dickens probed the giving of gifts in his *A Christmas Carol*. What changed in Scrooge to make him generous? What did his gifts express? Dickens wrote at the end of his story that Scrooge "knew how to keep Christmas well, if any man alive possessed the knowledge." Why? It is because a true gift has no strings attached, as our tax code says. It is also about the giving away of one's self, which our tax code does not comment on.

Wait in an expectant way. If no wondering takes place, don't worry. Each year wondering together will become more natural. Besides, just because people don't say things out loud does not mean that they are not wondering quietly to themselves.

Be supportive so that everyone who wants to speak has a chance. When the wondering is finished, say:

Our family is part of this story. Thanks be to God!

Put everything back into the box without hurrying. When everything is put back, the lid is replaced and the celebration is complete. Say:

Amen.

Conversation might continue as people leave the table.

Christmas Day

Pick up the box and look at it with interest and curiosity, then ceremoniously put it back on the table. Look at the people gathered and say:

Today is the moment we've been waiting for! It is time to enter the mystery of Christmas.

Move the box to one side and remove the lid. Place the box in the lid. Take out the model of Bethlehem and put it together. Place it on the table between you and the others.

Here is Bethlehem. Today we arrive with all those who have gone before us!

Take out the underlay and place it on the table to your right between you and the model of Bethlehem.

This changes everything, so the color changes from the color of getting ready to the color of pure celebration!

Unroll the panels as needed.

On the first Sunday in Advent, we remembered the prophets.

Place the first plaque.

On the second Sunday, we remembered Mary and Joseph as they made their way toward Bethlehem.

Place the second plaque.

On the third Sunday, we remembered the shepherds in the fields, keeping their flocks by night. They heard singing in the sky and saw a great light, so they ran to see the little king.

Place the third plaque.

On the fourth Sunday, we remembered how the *magi* adored the Christ Child and gave him gifts.

Place the fourth plaque.

Today we adore God's gift of God, as a little child, who changes us by the wonder of Christmas.

Place the fifth plaque on the white panel. Contemplate it for a moment, perhaps tracing the figures with your finger.

Now, I wonder if anyone in this family has ever become a gift?

Look at those who are gathered.
Invite them to speak, using your
manner as much as your words.

Support the possibility of wondering
for all who want to speak. When it
appears that the wondering is near
the end, say:

Our family is part of this story.
Thanks be to God!

Put everything back in the box with-
out hurrying. When everything is
put back, replace the lid and the
celebration is complete. Say:

Amen.

Conversation might continue after the
"Amen" as people linger or leave the table.

During the season of Advent and Christmas, you may want to leave the box on the table, so family members can wonder with it when they choose. You might also put it away to clear the table for other uses. Where you put the box and how you handle it is important, as mentioned above. It shows how much you value Christmas, your family, and the place of God's wondrous creativity of your home.

There is another choice you might need to make. Is there a way to incorporate the lighting of an Advent Wreath with the "storying" of Christmas? As you may have noticed, the Advent Wreath is pictured on all the plaques to integrate it with the story.

After the lid is placed on the box, the leader might say, "Now it is time to light the Advent Wreath." As you light the appropriate candle, thoughtfully say its name, such as "Today we light the candle of the prophets." After the candle for the day is lit, you say "Amen" to show the celebration is over. Come back later to extinguish the fire after the people have left the room.

Conclusion

Be easy on yourself as you "story" Christmas. The script and the objects will help your family and you weave together God's story and your family's stories. This may take some getting used to, but by the third year, if not immediately, most families look forward to this kind of "storying." The celebration will become more smooth and flexible as people get used to participating fully with grace and good humor. If this is not working smoothly after the third year, then try something else.

An alternative celebration might be to read Dickens's *A Christmas Carol* aloud. The importance of gathering the family around the table at Christmastime is the point. As you read Dickens aloud, the memories of your own Christmases are likely to find their way into your discussions of the reading. Notice that *A Christmas Carol* has five parts, or "staves" as Dickens called them, which fall neatly into one part for each of the Advent Sundays and the last one for reading on Christmas Day.

It is also good to try to go to church as a family on Christmas Eve.[5] Go out to eat as part of your celebration or have a feast at home as part of your family's Christmas tradition, if you can. If you can't get to church on Christmas Eve, see if there is a service on Christmas Day. It is usually a quiet, contemplative service without many people or much music.

The reason to go to church is to feel the reality of the larger community celebrating Christmas. The Church is a family of families of which you are a part, whether you can or want to attend worship or not. If you can't make it, then keeping Christmas at home will still deepen and broaden the celebration for your family and strengthen your family's ability to meet future challenges.

In the next chapter we will talk about Easter with all of its complications and beauty. The focus will be on how "to story" Easter at home and weave this celebration together with the story of your family.

---

5. The thought of "going to church" stimulates reactions in people from aversion to apathy as well as energized participation. The majority of the religiously unaffiliated are called "nones," because they check that box on questionnaires about church affiliation. They make up 25 percent of the American population. Only 7 percent of the nones say they are looking for a religious affiliation. Most have not been angered by their experience of the church or its stance on social issues. They just "stopped believing." Despite this, 1 in 3 of the nones believe children should be raised in a religion to learn "good values" and more than half say they believe in some "concept" of God. This information was summarized in the article "Most of the Unaffiliated Just 'Stopped Believing,' According to New Study" (*Christian Century*, October 26, 2016), 16–17.

CHAPTER 3

The Story of God's Re-Creative Love

Easter

Do you find Easter more complicated "to celebrate" than Christmas? I do. Do the symbols, strange stories, and liturgical action in the church stir deep and complex feelings or just put you off? Sometimes without fully realizing it we try to avoid all the "drama" by turning Easter into pastel greeting cards, spring flowers, chocolate bunnies, and plastic eggs. This makes it light and fun, which I love too, but getting rid of the Jesus stuff gets rid of Easter because Easter *is Jesus*. It is his story, not a concept.

There are many questions we might ask about Easter, but instead let's consider what Easter asks us. It asks, who are we, really? To answer this, we need to strike a balance between being too serious and not serious enough. We need to integrate the awful reality of Holy Week and the wonder of Easter Sunday to reveal our true identity and how to find it when it is lost.

The Questions
Easter Asks

Easter asks us to consider that Jesus could have fled into the hills and disappeared at any moment. Why did he choose to keep moving toward Jerusalem and his death? He wanted to give his life to show us how to transcend the life we feel confined in.

Our confinement is like living in a door-less room with four walls made from paradoxes. We are born to die. We crave meaning, but since *we* make it we mistrust it. We crave company but it absorbs us and we return to aloneness. We also seek freedom until we realize that we have it. We then flee rather than taking responsibility for our actions. The four walls confine us but above are the stars.

We can rise above our existential limits to be with God above, as well as beside and within us in the room. When our wholeness includes the Creator's creativity we can create justice and help God re-create us with grace. If we can experience the pain Jesus felt in his aloneness, absolute freedom, temporary loss of meaning on the cross, and death during Holy Week and integrate those feelings with the limitless horizon of Easter morning, then the creative process we were born with will flourish rather than being left behind, woefully underdeveloped. This is why it is important "to story" Easter with our families.

The stakes are high. If we allow our existential limits (Easter Week) and our openness (Easter) to separate, then the creative process will dissipate and no longer flow. Our deep identity will become a dry, empty valley of bones between two barren hills. This is because structure and openness are an unstable mixture and need each other for us to flow with God's creative energy.

But how does Easter talk about our deep identity? It is hard to hear because its way of speaking is odd. We need to listen carefully. God talk is not like science talk. It has its own goal and rules to reach that goal, which is to reveal who we truly are. Let me tell you a story about how to hear what Easter has to say.

A young child, only 3½ years old and his father were talking about God, death, and being too literal about God-talk. The late John M. Hull recorded this conversation and others in *God-Talk with Young Children* (1991). As often happens in such conversations, it began far from theology, but the God-talk soon emerged.

CHILD	Was that man's name Mr. Bird?
PARENT	Yes.
CHILD	Was he a bird? (Laughs)
PARENT	Was he like a bird?
CHILD	No.
PARENT	Why not?
CHILD	Birds have feathers. (Laughs)
PARENT	And the man didn't have feathers did he? He had clothes. (Both laugh.)
CHILD	And birds have wings.
PARENT	Yes.
CHILD	Birds die.
PARENT	So do people.
CHILD	(Silence)
PARENT	What does "die" mean?
CHILD	You go to be with God.

PARENT	Where is God?
CHILD	Up in the sky.
PARENT	But up in the sky there are clouds.
CHILD	(Laughs) No but I mean when you go up and up and up past the clouds and you go (speaking in a little high thin voice) up and up and up and then you come (whispering) to a teeny cottage and in that cottage there's God.

The child knew perfectly well that there was something strange about locating God up in the sky, so he showed that the word "sky" was symbolic by piling up the words he had at his disposal to say what he meant. When he realized that this strategy was insufficient, he changed the tone of his voice to add another symbolic layer to point beyond language toward the mystery of God's presence.

You can feel the playfulness in this conversation, which enabled the child to experiment with his big idea about God. This stimulated the whole child's knowing of the spirit by contemplation, his knowing of the body by the senses, and his knowing of his mind by reasoning with words. The quick wit and genuine delight in playing with God-talk on both sides of the generational gap enabled the father and son to create existential meaning together.

It may seem unusual to be so playful when talking about God and death, but this encouraged the flow of the creative process to make existential meaning. The laughter confirmed their engagement with the creative process and their delight in making meaning together.

This sort of conversation is indispensable for children's maturation and for hearing what Easter has to say. Let's talk about maturation first. When God-talk with children does not engage the creative process through play, children's use of religious language begins to fall behind the use of language in other areas of their development. Sometimes without intending to, we shut down the development of children's religious language skills. The resulting lag in development is not just a matter of vocabulary. It is *the use of religious language to make existential meaning* that falls behind rather than remembering theological words or passages from the Bible.

Learning Christian language through face-to-face conversations, like that of John Hull and his son, teaches Christian language *while learning how to use it*. Christian language is the language of love, so it needs to be learned with love, which involves our whole being.

What Easter has to say is that our deep identity involves us totally. We have sought wholeness as human beings since our species traveled in small bands to stay alive. Cave paintings and other artifacts show how we used mime, dance, and gestures to communicate this yearning as we developed language and language developed us.

Like our ancestors we also have a personal pre-linguistic time as infants. During that time we become adept at using the knowing of the spirit by contemplation to absorb God and the world around us in an undifferentiated way. We also use the knowing of the body by the senses to notice patterns in the world and within us. The knowing of our minds by reason and words is built on this non-verbal foundation. The Hebrew sages put our yearning for wholeness into the poetry of Genesis, which included the Creator as part of it. The affinity between the Creator and God's image within us completes the wholeness of who we are.

This brings us to Easter's answer to its own question. Who are we, *really*? We are creative creatures who create with others. Our wholeness includes our deep identity and God, but this affinity is always in danger of falling apart or being obscured. A surprising example of how we can regain who we truly are comes from Christmas, as we have already alluded to. Let's approach Easter's question and answer by talking again about Ebenezer Scrooge. This is because Dickens was very artful in his description of how Scrooge was redeemed by the wonder his meditation on the past, present, and future aroused.

Dickens expressed the experience of wonder that Scrooge had experienced when he showed up at Fred's Christmas feast after going to church and greeting people in the streets with his newfound generosity and love. He exclaimed, "Wonderful party, wonderful games, wonderful unanimity, wonder-full happiness!" Scrooge's nighttime reflections on his life and death had aroused his wonder, which in turn opened the flow of the creative process, which resulted in his re-creation.

Marley, who had learned a thing or two about our need for redemption in his death wanderings, was the hero of the story, dragging his chains. He may have been dead as a "door-nail," these seven years, but he is the one who moved Scrooge to reexamine his life and death, which aroused his wonder, which had been suppressed. His true identity had been locked in the narrowness of his rigid taking rather than giving.

Redemption is real rather than "an undigested bit of beef, a blot of mustard, a crumb of cheese, a fragment of an underdone potato." But it takes some reflection about who we really are to reveal our wholeness and depth once again. Redemption helps us walk gracefully again with balance after falling into rigidity or chaos. Notice how the old Scrooge and the new Scrooge walked through the city. The difference is striking! The "squeezing, wrenching, grasping, scraping, clutching, covetous, old sinner" becomes someone who "knew how to keep Christmas well, if any man alive possessed the knowledge." Easter is about how we can move from self-centered grasping to open handed generosity.

As Scrooge traveled with the Ghost of Christmas Past, he thought, "I should have liked, I do confess, to have had the lightest licence of a child and yet to have been man enough to know its value." Scrooge had begun to miss the creative wholeness he had known as a child with God. In the reexamination of his life and death, he realized that becoming like a child *really can lead* to the maturity beyond the norm Jesus referred to when he spoke about becoming like a child to enter God's kingdom.

As his book drew to a close, Dickens observed, "Some people laughed to see the alteration in him, but he let them laugh, and little heeded them; for he was wise enough to know that nothing happened on this globe, for good, at which some people did not have their fill of laughter at the outset . . . and knowing that such as these would be blind anyway. . . . His own heart laughed; and that was quite enough for him."

When Tiny Tim observed, "God bless Us, Every One," he was uttering an Easter as well as a Christmas blessing. Scrooge's redemption had been brought about directly by Marley's ghost, a holy spirit working for redemption. And indirectly by Tiny Tim, the humble but very strong Christ figure, whose eloquence and power was in his manner.

Scrooge is a familiar and vivid example of how we can go astray and yet recover our wholeness. His spirit-knowing and body-knowing had withered from lack of use and his knowing of the mind by reason had shriveled up within the narrow limits of speaking and thinking only about buying and selling without regard for others or even his own deep self. Scrooge had lost touch with his child-like identity as a creator. To help avoid this loss in our own families, let's turn now to "storying" Easter at home.

"Storying" Easter

The material for "storying" Easter comes in a box with a purple cross on it. The purple cross emphasizes the dark and serious time of preparing for Easter. The white cross of Easter can't be fully understood without passing through the dark time of the color purple.

Inside the box is a cloth underlay made of felt and the plaques to put on it, but this time the strip is unrolled toward those around the table instead of from the leader's right to left as in Creation and Christmas. The plaques picture seven faces of Christ. The underlay is a purple and white "scroll" that unrolls toward the group to show the six purple Sundays for Lent and a white one for Easter. When the scroll is rolled up, the light of Easter is inside the dark time of preparing. Like with the other stories of God, you need to consider carefully where to keep the box. Like the other materials, this one is available from Godly Play Resources, which is part of the non-profit Godly Play Foundation.

You can read more about the larger, classical version of this presentation in *The Complete Guide to Godly Play, Volume 4: Revised and Expanded.* It is used in Godly Play rooms in churches, schools, and other settings around the world and is called "The Faces of Easter." If your children participate in a Godly Play program, this presentation will recall what is done in the Godly Play room, but it is different enough to be interesting as well as familiar.

A problem with unrolling the scroll toward those gathered is that the rolled-up part can obscure the plaques. To avoid this, keep the roll close to you and hold on to it. Pull the next section out toward those watching and listening. It is as if the story of Lent and Easter is growing out from Jesus'

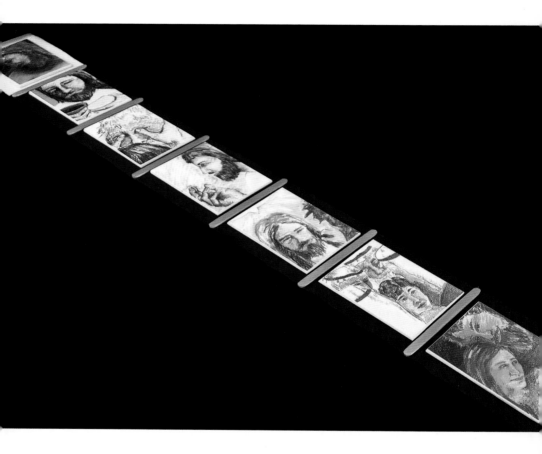

birth and the storyteller's life. Each Sunday the previous plaques are placed on the underlay and briefly mentioned to build toward the one for the day.

A good time and place to present this material is each Sunday in Lent and on Easter at the family table, but your family needs to decide what is best. A parent, aunt or uncle, grandparent, child, or other leader needs to be informally but clearly in charge. The leader's firm manner and sense of humor allows everyone to relax and participate in the movements and words. The leader also makes sure that everyone feels free to speak and no one overly dominates the wondering. When the family stories begin to lose their energy during the wondering, the leader says "Amen," and puts the material away to conclude the celebration while the participants are still interested.

What to Do and What to Say

The First Sunday in Lent

MOVEMENTS	WORDS
Pick up the box, which has already been placed on the table. Look at it with curiosity, then ceremoniously put it back on the table. Look at the people gathered and quietly say with energy and focus:	Today is the first Sunday in Lent. This is the time when we prepare to enter the mystery of Easter.
Move the box to one side and remove the lid. Put the box inside the lid. Take out the underlay and place it on the table in front of you.	This is the time of the color purple. It is the color of kings and queens, a serious and sometimes sad color. It is the color of getting ready.
Place one hand on the roll of the underlay and pull out the first section toward those gathered. Take the first plaque out of the box and hold it with two hands. Show it to the others. Trace the curves of the faces as you speak.	Today we remember how the baby was born.

Place the first plaque on the underlay, pause, and then lean toward those gathered, smiling.

Now, I wonder if anyone in this family was ever born? I wonder what that great day was like?

Participate in the storytelling, but keep alert to helping support everyone's participation. When everyone has had a chance to speak, you say:

Our family is part of this story. Thanks be to God!

Put everything back into the box without hurrying. When everything is returned, replace the lid to complete the celebration.

Amen.

Conversation may continue as people leave the table.

The Second Sunday in Lent

Pick up the box, look at it with curiosity, then ceremoniously place it back on the table. Look at the people gathered and quietly say, speaking with energy and focus:

Today is the second Sunday in Lent. This is the time when we prepare to enter the mystery of Easter.

Move the box to one side. Place it in the lid, then take out the underlay and place it on the table in front of you.

This is the time of the color purple, the color of kings and queens. It is a serious and sometimes sad color. It is the color of getting ready.

Place one hand on the roll of the underlay and pull out the first section toward the other people.

On the first Sunday in Lent, we remembered how the baby was born.

Place the first plaque on the underlay.

Pull out the second section and pick up the second plaque. Hold it with two hands while you talk about it and trace the figures.

Today we remember how the baby grew. When he was about twelve years old, he and his family went to Jerusalem for one of the high holy days. When it was time to go home, his parents could not find him. They looked everywhere. Finally, they looked in the Temple and there he was! He was talking to the Temple priests.

Place the second plaque on the underlay. Look at those gathered. Lean towards them and ask with invitation and curiosity:

Now, I wonder if anyone in this family was ever lost?

Support the responses, then when they begin to quiet, continue by saying:

I wonder if there was anyone who was ever found?

Participate in the "storying," but your first responsibility is to support the participation of the others. When everyone has had a chance to speak who wishes to, you say:

Our family is part of this story. Thanks be to God!

Return the plaques to the box in reverse order, roll up the underlay, and put it away. Replace the lid to complete the celebration. Say:

Amen.

Additional conversation may begin as people leave the table.

The Third Sunday in Lent

Pick up the box and look at it with curiosity and wonder. Place it ceremoniously back on the table. Say quietly but with energy and focus:

Today is the third Sunday in Lent. This is the time when we prepare to enter the mystery of Easter.

Move the box to one side and place it in the lid. Take out the underlay and place it on the table in front of you.

This is the time of the color purple. It is the color of kings and queens. It is a serious and sometimes sad color. It is the color of getting ready.

Pull out the sections of the underlay as needed. Hold the plaques for a moment as you reflect on them, then place them on the underlay.

On the first Sunday in Lent, we remembered how the baby was born.

On the second Sunday, we remembered how the child was lost and found.

Hold the third plaque while you trace how it shows Jesus' baptism. Say:

Today we remember how Jesus was baptized in the River Jordan.

Pause for a moment to let the image and the words sink in.

Now, I wonder if anyone in this family was ever baptized? I wonder what that was like?

Your attitude about the wondering is important. Support those gathered by inviting them to speak if they wish. It is good to contribute to the stories, but don't overly dominate the conversation. As the wondering draws to a close, say:

Our family is part of this story. Thanks be to God!

Put everything back into the box without hurrying. When everything is replaced, put the lid on the box. The celebration is complete. Say:

Amen.

Conversation may continue as people leave the table.

The Fourth Sunday in Lent

Pick up the box and look at it with curiosity and wonder, then place it ceremoniously back on the table. Look at the people who are gathered, and say:

Today is the fourth Sunday in Lent. This is the time when we prepare to enter the mystery of Easter.

Move the box to one side. Take off the lid. Place the box in the lid. Take out the underlay and place it in front of you.

This is the time of the color purple. It is the color of kings and queens. It is a serious and sometimes sad color. It is the color of getting ready.

Pull out each section as needed and place the appropriate plaque on it.

On the first Sunday in Lent, we remembered how the baby was born.

On the second Sunday in Lent, we remembered how the child was lost and found.

On the third Sunday in Lent, we remembered how Jesus was baptized.

Hold the current plaque with both hands with the picture toward those gathered. Trace the figures as you say:

Today we remember how Jesus went into the desert to discover who he was and what his work was going to be.

Lay the plaque on the underlay.

Now, I wonder if anyone in our family has ever wondered who they are or what their work is going to be?

Participate in, but primarily guide the storytelling and listening. When everyone has had a chance to speak, bring this part of the celebration to an end by saying:

Our family is part of this story. Thanks be to God!

*Put everything back into the box with-
out hurrying. When everything is back
inside, replace the lid and the celebration
is complete. Say:*

Amen.

*Conversation may continue as people
leave the table.*

The Fifth Sunday in Lent

*Pick up the box with curiosity and delight.
After wondering silently about it, put it
back on the table.*

Today is the fifth Sunday in Lent. This
is the time when we prepare to enter
the mystery of Easter.

*Move the box to one side and put the
box in the lid. Take out the underlay
and place it in front of you.*

This is the time of the color purple,
the color of kings and queens. It is a
serious and sometimes sad color. It is
the color of getting ready.

*Place one hand on the roll and pull
out the sections as needed. Place the
appropriate plaque on each one.*

On the first Sunday in Lent, we
remembered how the baby was born.

On the second Sunday in Lent, we
remembered how the child was lost
and found.

On the third Sunday in Lent, we
remembered how Jesus was baptized.

On the fourth Sunday in Lent, we
remembered how Jesus went into the
desert to discover who he was and
what his work was going to be.

Hold the plaque of the day with two hands, as you show it to the others. You then say:

Today we remember how Jesus began his work. But what was his work? He came close to people to heal them and he told parables to help them enter God's kingdom.

Place the plaque on the underlay.

Now, I wonder if anyone in our family ever came close to God or wondered what God's kingdom is like?

Be supportive of the wondering. If no wondering takes place, wait in an expectant way. Each year this part of "storying" will become more natural. It is always good to remember that just because people don't say anything out loud, it doesn't mean that they aren't wondering to themselves.

After everyone has spoken, who would like to speak, finish this part of the celebration by saying:

Our family is part of this story. Thanks be to God!

Put everything back into the box and replace the lid. This shows that the celebration is complete. Say:

Amen.

Conversation may continue as people leave the table.

The Sixth Sunday in Lent

Pick up the box and look at it with curiosity and wonder. Place the box back on the table with ceremony. Look at the people gathered. Speak slowly and quietly, but with energy and focus, as you say:

Today is the sixth Sunday in Lent. This is the time when we prepare to enter the mystery of Easter.

Move the box to one side and remove the lid. Put the box inside the lid. Take out the underlay and place it on the table in front of you.

This is the time of the color purple, the color of kings and queens. It is a serious and sometimes sad color. It is the color of getting ready.

Pull out the sections of the underlay and place the appropriate plaque on each one.

On the first Sunday in Lent, we remembered how the baby was born.

On the second Sunday, we remembered how the child was lost and found.

On the third Sunday, we remembered how Jesus was baptized.

On the fourth Sunday, we remembered how Jesus went into the desert to discover who he was and what his work was going to be.

On the fifth Sunday, we remembered how Jesus began his work. He came close to people to heal them and told parables to help them enter God's kingdom.

Hold the plaque with two hands as you show it to the others.

Today we remember how Jesus finally knew that he had to go to Jerusalem to become a parable. On Thursday in Holy Week, he shared the bread and wine for the last time with the Twelve.

Place the plaque on the underlay.

Pause for a moment. Take a deep breath and then say:

Now, I wonder if anyone in this family ever discovered something new when sharing the Holy Bread and the Holy Wine?

Guide the wondering. When the energy in the conversation begins to wind down, end this part of the process by saying:

Our family is part of this story. Thanks be to God!

Put everything back into the box and put the lid on it. Don't hurry. Do this with meditative intention. When everything is put away, the celebration is complete. Say:

Amen.

Conversation may continue as people leave the table.

Easter Sunday

Pick up the box, which has already been placed on the table. Look at it with curiosity and deep interest, then ceremoniously place it back on the table and say:

The time for getting ready is over. Today is the day we have been waiting for! Lent is done and Easter's begun.

Move the box to one side and remove the lid. Place the box in the lid. Take out the underlay and place it on the table in front of you.

The time of the color purple is over and the pure white of Easter light now appears.

Unroll the underlay, placing each plaque on the appropriate section, moving smoothly and quickly.

We remember
how the baby was born;
how the child was lost and found;
how Jesus was baptized;
how he went into the desert to discover who he was and what his work was going to be; how his work was coming close to people and telling parables; how he knew he had to become a parable; and how on that Thursday night he shared the bread and wine for the last time with the disciples.

Pull out the white section of the underlay. Show the crucified Christ to those gathered while you hold the plaque with two hands.

Jesus died on the cross for us and that is very sad . . .

Turn the plaque over to show the resurrected Christ on the other side, presenting the Bread and Wine.

. . . but somehow he is still with us, especially in the Bread and the Wine.

When you see this,

Show the crucified Christ.

you know this is there, too.
And when you see this,

Continue showing the risen Lord.

you know that this is also there.

Show the crucified Christ.

And you cannot pull them apart.

Turn the plaque sideways toward the family and pull on the wood with your fingers to show the faces cannot be separated.

That is the mystery of Easter.

Pause and reflect on the two faces. Turn the plaque over and over, then place it on the white section of the underlay with the Risen Christ, face up.

Now, I wonder if anyone in this family ever entered the mystery of Easter? I wonder what you found?

The wondering questions are designed to stimulate thinking. Let them do their work. Wait with patience for the wondering out loud to begin. If it does not, that's okay. This is a lot for people to process. When everyone has spoken who wishes to speak, say:

Our family is part of this story.
Thanks be to God!

Put everything back in the box without hurrying. Don't rush as you return the plaques to the box and name each one. Replace the lid.

(If you include the ringing of bells,
which will be explained in a moment,
do that now before the "Amen.")

The "storying" is now complete, so say: **Amen.**

Conversation may continue as people
leave the table.

Each time the "storying" is completed, you have a choice. You might leave the box on the table, so family members can wonder more with the material when they choose during Lent and Easter. You can also put the box away, where you keep your special Easter things, during the week until the next time you share the celebration.

There is nothing in the celebration of Easter quite like the Advent wreath of Christmas, but there is the custom of ringing bells. They are sometimes rung in church on Easter morning. This is why you might want to have a basket of bells on the table for Easter Sunday. The family can playfully ring in the joy of Easter as the celebration is drawing to a close. After the bells are rung, the leader says, "Amen."

As with Christmas, it is important to join others in church to celebrate Easter. There are jokes about people only going to church at Christmas and Easter, but there is no better time to go, and it is no joke. If you can go to church on other Sundays, then go, but if you can't, then make a special effort to worship in a community larger than your family on Christmas and Easter

Conclusion

So who are we, *really*? Easter speaks to us in its own unique way about our authenticity, which is related to our wholeness and deep identity as creators. The wholeness we seek involves our knowing of the spirit by contemplation, our knowing of the body by the senses, and our knowing of our mind by reason and words. Our wholeness also includes the Creator, whose creativity is found in us through God's image. Easter invites us to live our authentic identity as creators in the image of God and return to it when it is lost, which is a continuing danger. This is why it is important "to story" Easter with our family.

We have now looked at ways to celebrate Creation, Christmas, and Easter in the home. The next chapter is about "storying" Pentecost. It is generally the least known of the three great liturgical celebrations of the church, but the deep logic that links our participation in God's creation with the liturgies of Christmas, Easter, and Pentecost is worth reflecting on as the book moves forward.

CHAPTER 4

The Story of God Creating from Within

Pentecost

What is Pentecost? My family didn't observe this ancient Christian celebration as I was growing up, so I have no deep memories of it. As I grew older I wondered what it was about. What experience did it identify, name, value, and express in people's lives? Still later, during my theological training, I tried but failed to enter its mystery for a variety of reasons. Decades later I began to understand and realized how easy it is to miss the point of Pentecost. This chapter responds to such considerations as it invites you "to story" Pentecost with your family.

The Origin and Complexity of Pentecost

Pentecost was first associated with the Jewish celebration of *Shavuot* (Weeks), which was called 'Pentecost' (Fifty Days) by Greek-speaking Jews. Jews counted weeks or days from Passover to establish the day while Christians counted from their Easter.

In Acts we read how Paul sailed past Ephesus so he could be back in Jerusalem in time for the day of Pentecost (Acts 20:16). Another time he wrote to the Christians in Corinth that he wanted to come see them, but he planned to stay in Ephesus until Pentecost (1 Corinthians 16:8). It seems that Paul himself celebrated Pentecost although he may have been referring to his continued celebration of *Shavuot*.

Shavout remains a time of joy and sometimes dancing in the synagogue. It expresses gratitude for the grain harvest and the giving of the Torah on Mt. Sinai. The synagogue and home are decorated with greenery and flowers to remember, as tradition tells us, when the usually arid Mount Sinai suddenly blossomed with flowers at the giving of the Torah on its summit. The story of Ruth is read during the celebration because of its connection with her gleaning the grain from the harvest of Boaz, whom she later married. This marriage established the line that gave birth to King David, so the festival is important for many reasons to the Jewish People.

At the first Christian Pentecost Jews were streaming into Jerusalem to celebrate their Pentecost. They came from all over the world to observe the great day at the Temple. The disciples and other followers of Jesus were hidden away in an upper room during this time. They were waiting for the coming of the Holy Spirit, as Jesus promised on Ascension Day (Acts 1:3-11).

Suddenly, they felt the Holy Spirit enter the room with a sound like the rush of a mighty wind (Acts 2:1–13). It filled them with radiant energy, as they became aware of God's creative presence in and among them. It was in this way that their community transcended kinship and healed the division of languages, memorialized in the story of the "Tower of Babel" (Genesis 11:1–9). God's incandescent presence did not need words to communicate its inner and relational reality, which turned Jesus' followers (disciples) into leaders (apostles).

The "first fruits" of the harvest were offered to God at *Shavout*. Christians also used this phrase when they remembered Christ's sacrifice. Paul wrote to the Christians in Corinth that Jesus was the "first fruits" of the harvest (1 Corinthians 15:20–23). He died to bring new life, which suggests seedtime, ripening, and life coming out of death like when seeds are eaten or planted. This mystery began to be internalized by those in the upper room at Pentecost.

The festival of Pentecost for both Jews and Christians suggest that life comes out of death, even though death is profoundly real and absolutely personal. The Jewish and Christian meanings are not the same, because the symbols and stories are different, but there is an emotional affinity and wisdom that connects the two celebrations.

The people who were gathered in the upper room on the first Christian Pentecost were a mixed group. The disciples were there. There were also "certain women, including Mary the mother of Jesus, as well as his brothers" (Acts 1:14). There must have been many unmentioned women, men, and children present, as this first "family of families" became the church.

We long for and work towards the ideal Church born in Pentecost, but there is a great surplus of meaning that goes beyond calling this the birthday of the church. This is why we need to prepare carefully to enter the mystery of Pentecost, like we do for Christmas and Easter.

The time of preparing for Pentecost is called "Eastertide." It combines the continuing celebration of Easter with preparing for Pentecost. It remembers when the disciples and others began to know Jesus in a new way. During this process Jesus' followers discovered that he was neither simply human nor simply divine. He was completely both in a way that is anything but simple.

Jesus' appearances during the period between Easter and Pentecost have fascinated people from the disciples, to the opponents of the early Christians, to our own scientific-minded age. Whatever happened when the disciples experienced Jesus' new kind of presence, it was powerful. Paul, for example, was a committed opponent of the followers of Christ. He was on his way to Damascus to attack them when he experienced Jesus' presence along the road. This changed his life, as such experiences still change people's lives today.

Paul provided us with the earliest written list of appearances (1 Corinthians 15:3–11). He forgot, or may not have known about, the women at the empty tomb. The Gospel writers, who wrote after Paul, all included them in their accounts (Matthew 28:1–10; Mark 16:1–8; Luke 24:1–11; and John 20:1–10).

Mary Magdalene and other women had gone early to the tomb to finish preparing Jesus' body for burial. They found the tomb empty. Jesus then appeared to Mary Magdalene in the garden (John 20:11–18). She ran to tell Peter, who came running with "the other disciple, the one whom Jesus loved," who was, probably, John.

Paul's letter to the church in Corinth said that Jesus "appeared to Cephas, then to the twelve." He then noted that Jesus also appeared to "more than five hundred brethren at one time," as it says in various translations. The New Revised Standard Version, however, translates this "more than five hundred brothers and sisters at one time" (1 Corinthians 15:6) and then footnotes that the text actually only mentions the men. What is remarkable about this reasonable addition of women to the text is that children are still left out! If there were men and women gathered in those days, there must also have been children present. This is another reason why it is very important "to story" Pentecost at home with the whole family present.

"Storying" Pentecost

The material for "storying" Pentecost at home has the flame of Pentecost on the top of its box. Inside are six plaques with images showing the resurrection appearances of Jesus. There is also an underlay with six white

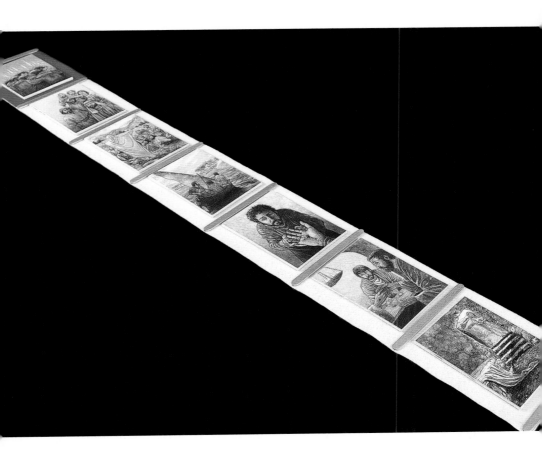

panels and one that is red, which is rolled up inside the white ones. This is a smaller version for the home of the classical Godly Play material for Pentecost.[1] This does not replace or update the classical one. It is merely used for a different purpose.

This presentation begins where the "Faces of Easter" ends, so the white of Easter is placed at an arm's length from the leader. It is then unrolled back toward the leader. The story of Jesus, which was unrolled from the leader outward, now moves back toward the leader, as if the story were being internalized by experiencing Jesus in a new way. There is no need to

1. Jerome W. Berryman, *The Complete Guide to Godly Play, Volume* 8 (Denver: Morehouse Educational Resources, 2012), 80–131.

talk about this. Just tell the story and see if anyone notices and wants to talk about this difference. It is a wondering waiting to happen. The presentation ends with a change of color from the white of Eastertide to the red of Pentecost.

What to Do and What to Say

MOVEMENTS	WORDS
Pick up the box. Look at it with appreciation and curiosity, then place it ceremoniously back on the table. Look at those gathered and speak quietly but with energy and focus:	This is the time when we prepare to enter the mystery of Pentecost. It is called "Eastertide."
Move the box to one side and remove the lid. Put the box inside the lid. Take out the underlay and place it on the table in front of you about an arm's length away.	This is the time of the color white.[2] Easter is so great a mystery that it can't be kept in one Sunday, so it keeps on going for six weeks and helps us prepare for Pentecost.
Unroll the underlay toward you, leaving the first panel easily seen by the others.	Today is the first Sunday in Eastertide.

---

2. The phrase "color white" refers to the balanced combination of blue, red, and yellow, the primary colors. When light enters the eyes and stimulates all three types of color-sensitive cone cells in equal amounts, we experience "white." White light is produced electronically by projecting a mixture of blue, red, and yellow at full intensity. Black is the experience of no color. The color white, then, suggests that Easter is a truth that metaphorically incorporates everything.

Pick up the first plaque and hold it with two hands while you show it to the others.

Today we remember how Jesus was not in the tomb. He was known in a new way by not being there!

Pause. Gather yourself and then begin to lead the wondering.

Now, I wonder if there is anyone in our family who died and yet is still with us?

Like all the wonderings, this one invites reflection. Wait in an expectant way for people to respond. When everyone has had a chance to speak, you say:

Our family is part of this story. Thanks be to God!

Put the plaque in the box, roll up the underlay, and put it away. Replace the lid to conclude the celebration by saying:

Amen.

Conversation might continue as people leave the table.

The Second Sunday in Eastertide

Pick up the box. Look at it with interest and appreciation, then place it ceremoniously back on the table. Look at those gathered, then speak openly and with energy:

This is the time when we prepare to enter the mystery of Pentecost. It is called "Eastertide."

Move the box to one side and remove the lid. Put the box inside the lid. Take out the underlay and place it on the table in front of you about an arm's length away.

This is the time of the color white. Easter is so great a mystery that it can't be kept in one Sunday, so it keeps on going for six weeks and helps us prepare for Pentecost.

Pick up the first plaque and show it to the others.

On the first Sunday in Eastertide, we remembered how Jesus was known in absence.

Place the first plaque on the underlay. Unroll the underlay toward you, revealing the second section.

Pick up the second plaque and hold it with two hands, showing it to the others while you speak, perhaps tracing the figures.

Today we remember how Jesus met two people on the road to Emmaus. They talked about the Bible with Jesus as they walked, but they did not recognize him. He was made known to them in the breaking of bread when they had supper together.

Place the second plaque and then gather yourself for the wondering. Look at those around the table.

Now, I wonder if there is anyone in our family who was better known by breaking bread with them?

Like all the wonderings, this one invites reflection. Wait in an expectant way for people to respond. When everyone has had a chance to speak, you say:

Our family is part of this story. Thanks be to God!

Put everything back in the box and replace the lid. Say:

Amen.

Conversations might continue as people leave the table.

The Third Sunday in Eastertide

Pick up the box. Look at it with amazement, like you have never seen it before, then place it with ceremony back on the table.

This is the time when we prepare to enter the mystery of Pentecost. It is called "Eastertide."

Move the box to one side and remove the lid. Put the box inside the lid. Take out the underlay and place it on the table in front of you about an arm's length away.

This is the time of the color white. Easter is so great a mystery that it can't be kept in one Sunday, so it keeps on going for six weeks and helps us prepare for Pentecost.

Unroll the first section of the underlay.

On the first Sunday of Eastertide, we remembered how Jesus was known in absence.

Unroll the second section of the under-lay and place the second card as you say:

On the second Sunday of Eastertide, we remembered how Jesus was known in the breaking bread.

Unroll the third section of the underlay. Pick up the third plaque and hold it with two hands as you speak.

Today we remember how Thomas doubted that Jesus was really there.

Place the third plaque, then pause. Gather yourself. Begin the wondering:

Now, I wonder if there is anyone in this family who ever doubted things?

Wait a moment to see if anyone will respond. Wait expectantly. Sometimes it is good to share your own experiences to get the wondering started. When the wondering subsides, say:

Our family is part of this story. Thanks be to God!

Put the images in the box. Roll up the underlay, and put it away. Put the lid back on the box to show that the celebration is complete. Say:

Amen.

Conversation might continue as people leave the table.

The Fourth Sunday in Eastertide

Pick up the box. Look at it with appreciation and curiosity, then place it ceremoniously back on the table. Look at those gathered and speak quietly but with energy and focus:

This is the time we prepare to enter the mystery of Pentecost. It is called "Eastertide."

Move the box to one side and remove the lid. Put the box inside the lid. Take out the underlay and place it on the table in front of you about an arm's length away.

This is the time of the color white. Easter is so great a mystery that it can't be kept in one Sunday, so it keeps on going for six weeks and helps us prepare for Pentecost.

Unroll the first section of the underlay towards you and place the first card as you say:

On the first Sunday in Eastertide, we remembered how Jesus was known in absence.

Unroll the second section of the underlay and place the second card. Move smoothly and quickly as the previous days are remembered.

On the second Sunday in Eastertide, we remembered how Jesus was known in the breaking of bread.

Unroll the third section of the underlay and place the third card.

On the third Sunday in Eastertide, we remembered how Jesus was known by doubting.

Unroll the fourth section of the underlay. Pick up the fourth card and hold it. Trace the figures as you say:

Today we remember how Jesus was known in the morning as he cooked breakfast by the Sea of Galilee.

Place the fourth card, then pause and gather yourself for the wondering:

Now, I wonder if there is anyone in our family who was ever known better by doing ordinary things with them?

Wait in an expectant way to see if anyone will respond. Sometimes it is good to offer something from your own experience to encourage wondering. If there is silence or when the wondering loses its energy, conclude by saying:

Our family is part of this story. Thanks be to God!

Put all the images back in the box, roll up the underlay, and put it away. The lid is replaced and the celebration is concluded. Say:

Amen.

Conversations might continue as people leave the table.

The Fifth Sunday in Eastertide

Pick up the box. Look at it with appreciation and curiosity, then place it with dignity back on the table. Look at those gathered and speak slowly with emphasis on each word:

This is the time we prepare to enter the mystery of Pentecost. It is called "Eastertide."

Set down the box and move it to one side. Remove the lid and place the box in it. Take out the underlay and place it an arm's length away.

This is the time of the color white. Easter is so great a mystery that it can't be kept in one Sunday, so it keeps on going for six weeks and helps us prepare for Pentecost.

Unroll the first section of the underlay and place the first card.

On the first Sunday of Eastertide, we remembered how Jesus was known in absence.

Unroll the second section of the underlay and place the second card.

On the second Sunday of Eastertide, we remembered how Jesus was known in the breaking of bread.

Unroll the third section of the underlay and place the third card.

On the third Sunday of Eastertide, we remembered how Jesus was known in doubt.

Unroll the fourth section of the underlay and place the fourth card.

On the fourth Sunday of Eastertide, we remembered how Jesus was known in doing ordinary things.

Unroll the fifth section of the underlay and hold the fifth card for a moment with both hands to show your appreciation. As you hold it, say:

Today we remember how Jesus told the disciples on a mountain in Galilee to make his story real by living it and by baptizing people.

Place the fifth card. Gather yourself for the wondering and say:

Now, I wonder if there is anyone in this family who knows how to make a story real?

Like all the wonderings, this one invites reflection. Wait in an expectant way for the others to respond. When everyone has had a chance to speak, say:

Our family is part of this story. Thanks be to God!

Put the plaques in the box, roll up the underlay, and put it away. Replace the lid and complete the celebration by saying:

Amen.

Conversations might continue as people leave the table.

The Sixth Sunday in Eastertide

Pick up the box. Look at it with appreciation and curiosity, then place it ceremoniously back on the table. Look at those gathered, then say quietly but with energy and focus:

This is the time we prepare to enter the mystery of Pentecost. It is called "Eastertide."

Move the box to one side and remove the lid. Put the box inside the lid. Take out the underlay and place it on the table in front of you about an arm's length away.

This is the time of the color white. Easter is so great a mystery that it can't be kept in one Sunday, so it keeps on going for six weeks and helps us prepare for Pentecost.

Unroll the first section of the underlay and place the first card.

On the first Sunday in Eastertide, we remembered how Jesus was known in absence.

Unroll the second section of the underlay toward you and place the second card.

On the second Sunday in Eastertide, we remembered how Jesus was known in the breaking of bread.

Unroll the third section of the underlay toward you and place the third card.

On the third Sunday in Eastertide, we remembered how Jesus was known in doubt.

Unroll the fourth section of the underlay toward you and place the fourth card.

On the fourth Sunday in Eastertide, we remembered how Jesus was known in doing ordinary things.

Unroll the fifth section of the underlay toward you and place the fifth card.

On the fifth Sunday in Eastertide, we remembered how Jesus was known by living his story.

Unroll the sixth section and pick up the sixth plaque. Hold it with two hands and silently contemplate it, perhaps, tracing the images on it.

Today we remember how Jesus was known in saying goodbye.

Place the card and then prepare yourself to begin the wondering by saying:

Now, I wonder if there is anyone in our family who was ever known better in the saying of goodbye?

Like all the wonderings, this one invites reflection. Wait in an expectant way for people to respond. When everyone has had a chance to speak, say:

Our family is part of this story. Thanks be to God!

Put the plaques in the box, roll up the underlay, and put it away. Replace the lid to complete the "storying."

Amen.

Conversations might continue as people leave the table.

Pentecost Sunday

Pick up the box. Look at it with appreciation and curiosity, then place it ceremoniously back on the table. Look at those gathered and say with energy and focus:

Today is Pentecost, fifty days after Easter. This is the day we have been waiting for!

Move the box to one side and remove the lid. Put the box inside the lid. Take out the underlay and place it on the table in front of you about an arm's length away.

The followers were all together in one place. Suddenly, there was a sound, like the rush of a mighty wind. It filled the room, and fire was within each one, so the color of Pentecost is red.

This was when they stopped following and began leading, because the Creator was known within each one to sustain them all.

Unroll the sections of the underlay. Touch each one of the cards as you smoothly place them on the panels, saying what each one stands for. Finally, pause and then show the plaque for Pentecost to the others.

Jesus is still known in absence. Jesus is still known in the breaking of bread. Jesus is still known in doubt. Jesus is still known in doing ordinary things. Jesus is still known in living his story. Jesus is still known in saying goodbye, and Jesus is still known in the coming of the Holy Spirit to renew us.

Sit back. Pause while reflecting on the whole layout in front of you. Touch each card. Begin the wondering by saying:

I wonder if anyone in our family ever feels like something new is being created within?

This wondering invites reflection, but you may encounter silence. Wait with openness. Sometimes it helps if you share some of your own experience, but this can also inhibit further wondering. Be sure that all who wish to speak have a chance to speak, then say:

Our family is part of this story. Thanks be to God!

Put the images back in the box, roll up
the underlay, and put it away. Replace
the lid. This shows that the celebration
is complete. You then say: **Amen.**

Conversations might continue as people
leave the table.

This family presentation may take a bit more preparation than the others, because the story is not as familiar as Christmas and Easter. The rhythm of the presentation, however, is familiar, which will help, and the pictures on the plaques will prompt you.

As with the celebrations of Christmas and Easter, it is important to try to go to church on Pentecost Sunday to feel the community of the church worshiping all around the world. There is also a touch of good humor about this. People may be surprised to know that you are taking Pentecost as seriously as Christmas and Easter. Many don't realize that celebrating Creation, Christmas, Easter, and Pentecost are part of a single process that leads to human growth and development.

It is also good at this time to remember that Pentecostals, who emphasize the coming of the Holy Spirit, are as many as 270 million strong worldwide. They continue to experience great growth, especially in the global south. What is interesting is that Pentecostals don't make much if anything about Pentecost Sunday. This is because they celebrate each day as Pentecost, which is a lesson for all of us. We need to always be aware, like the Pentecostals, that the Holy Spirit can enter our lives at any moment and that this integration can lead to being leaders instead of followers.

Still, it is easy to miss the point of Pentecost, as I discovered several times growing up. Let's discuss it a bit more, to honor the richness of this great biblical and liturgical event so it can be more fully appreciated at home.

Missing the Point
about Pentecost

What is the point of Pentecost? The point is to celebrate God's creative image within us, and how this image can be rediscovered by the power of the Holy Spirit when lost. Re-experiencing God in creation, celebrating wonder in Christmas, knowing the faith, hope, and love of redemption in Easter, and the internalization of this whole process in Pentecost can lead to our becoming spiritually integrated leaders rather than followers, as happened to the disciples.

We sometimes miss the point of Pentecost because the drama of Jesus' appearances distracts us. We get diverted in roughly four ways. First, some think the appearances are "factually true," but for the wrong reasons. Others think they are not true, so they try to explain what happened in naturalistic terms. A third group misses the point by shrinking the meaning of the appearances to illustrations of how Jesus is God. A final distraction is the reduction of the appearances to celebrating "the birthday of the church." Reducing Pentecost to a birthday cake misses the creative power of its mystery. Let's discuss each of these distractions a bit more.

First, the debate about the historical or scientific truth of the appearances distracts us from the significance of the variety of the appearances and how that forces us to see the richness of what it means to be alive and how that is to be understood. The appearances don't prove that Jesus was God because only God could suspend the natural order for these occurrences to take place. That sort of discussion is brittle and of little use to the living of our days. What *is* of use is to realize that we can be "present" in a great variety of ways, which opens our mind to a richer view of life and death.

We also miss a related point about Pentecost by narrowing its meaning to something we can express in a naturalistic, scientific way. Some assume out of hand that the stories about Jesus' appearances didn't really happen. They still love the Bible, so they try to explain away the appearances in a naturalistic way to validate the "facts" of the appearances. The leading "explanation" for the appearances is psychological. It goes something like this: the disciples missed Jesus deeply and longed to see him so much that they imagined he was there around every corner and on every mountain-top. Of course people missed Jesus! They continued wondering about the Easter event, as we do today, so they celebrated the variety of ways Jesus was or could be known. This wonder was an extension of the question Easter asks us about our human nature. Who are we, *really*?

A third way we sometimes miss the point about Jesus' appearances is to ignore their historical and psychological reality and turn them into illustrations of how Jesus is God. Sometimes people think about the appearances as if they were like Aesop's fables. Aesop (620–564 BCE) was a Greek fable-maker who may have been a Greek slave from Ethiopia. He collected and wrote fables for wise people to discuss and learn from. By the Renaissance, however, the translations of Aesop's fables began to be addressed to children to teach them morality. Each fable was tagged with a concise moral statement to be memorized. The story's complex richness was dismissed and turned into an illustration of the moralism to be taught. The original Greek versions of the tales were points of departure for learning more rather than arrival to stop thinking and start memorizing, which is a good way to think about the Gospels' stories of Jesus' appearances.

The fourth way to miss the point about Pentecost is to reduce its meaning to history. We can all agree that Pentecost was the beginning of the church because this is a historical fact, supported by the biblical texts, and because there is nothing problematic or unscientific about such an interpretation. The trouble with this minimal meaning is that it relegates Pentecost to the past and ignores its relevance to us today for discovering our deepest identity in the Creator's image.

All four of these misunderstandings may come from not fully appreciating what the Gospel writers and their readers had in mind when they wrote and read at the turn of the first century. The gospel stories are a mixture of what was experienced by those who were present at the appearances, their interpretation of what that experience meant for them, and the use of symbolic language to express what happened. This kind of communication is different from our views of science and history today, but it is inappropriate to dismiss it for that reason. The first century writers and readers did not think their approach needed to be revised or dismissed. They thought it was needed to get inside the meaning of the appearances to find what is nourishing, just like the nourishing part of an egg is what's inside the egg-shell. We need to taste, savor, and digest the egg, not just describe it from the outside for it to make a difference in our lives.

The gospel writers were writing about Jesus in a traditional, Jewish way. They were telling stories and then *telling stories about the stories they told* to help the listeners interpret, expand, and apply them to their lives. Those listening to the stories understood this, and in some cases we do not. The appearances created a network of stories for readers and listeners to discover the personal, interpretive, and symbolic truth, which is embodied in the narrative art of the Creation-Christmas-Easter-Pentecost experience.

Conclusion

The origin and complexity of Pentecost needs to be acknowledged for us to enter into its mystery. To know Jesus in this new way, we need to be aware of the many angles and levels of interpretation involved. Jesus was and is known in absence, in the breaking of bread, in doubt, in the doing of ordinary things, in our living out the story of his life, in saying goodbye, and in the rushing wind and fire of the Holy Spirit entering our lives. Understanding Pentecost in this complex way helps us know more broadly and deeply who we are and how to become creative and integrated spiritual leaders instead of dependent, rigid followers of the latest enthusiasm or chaotic deniers of our deep identity.

We have now "storied" and wondered about Creation, Christmas, Easter, and Pentecost. This brings us to the next story of God. It involves Jesus' story about himself. It is in part an "I-Am" story from John's Gospel, but it also involves a parable, told by Jesus about the lost sheep, a story about seeking God and God seeking us. Echoes of the Twenty-Third Psalm can also be heard singing in it.

CHAPTER 5

The Story of God's Caring and Creative Presence

The Good Shepherd

Knowing God is odd. There is no place to stand outside God to get perspective on what we are looking at. This is why we need to know God from within our relationship with the Creator. Telescopes and microscopes are useless, so we need to use the theological method rather than the scientific method. The theological method involves liturgical action, contemplative silence, parables, and sacred stories to know God, who comes to us continually from beyond, beside, and within as the creator. As in any endeavor, we need to use the right tools for the job to know God.

The story of God we will use to know God in this chapter involves a mixture of the Twenty-Third Psalm, an "I-Am" statement from John's Gospel where Jesus identified himself as the Good Shepherd (John 10:1–18), and a parable he told about a lost sheep (Matthew 18:12–14 and Luke 15:3–7). The only trouble with this approach is that if you are not steeped in the Bible or live in a sheep-raising community, these stories may seem irrelevant or strange at best. This is why we need to begin by discussing how to make meaning with stories about sheep and shepherds.

The Strangeness and Relevance of Stories about Sheep and Shepherds

I have been ambivalent about thinking of God in terms of sheep and shepherds since I was a child. This is partly because I grew up in cattle country in Western Kansas. The old rumors about sheep cropping the prairie grass so short that it died out or that sheep left a scent on the grass that stopped the cattle from eating it were still around as I was growing up. Both rumors if true would have endangered the great cattle herds of the late nineteenth century that grazed the open range before the invention of barbed wire, but that was long ago and the rumors weren't true. The cattlemen didn't care. They did not like sheep and shepherds. The term "deadline" came from those early days. If the sheepherders and their flocks crossed a line drawn in the grass by the cattlemen, they were dead.

I also remember as a child gazing up at a stained glass window in our church. The glass showed impossibly green grass, very blue water, and wooly, white sheep. I was vaguely aware of how this contrasted with the brown buffalo grass, scarce water in the sandy creeks, and the white-faced Hereford cattle in my world. Still, there was something peaceful and illuminating about the stained glass, so when it came time to memorize the Twenty-Third Psalm, I did so gladly. As I grew older, the contradiction faded but so did the psalm. Decades later I memorized the psalm again so I could always have it with me. I had rediscovered what people have known for thousands of years. It can "restoreth the soul."

The Twenty-Third Psalm invites us to know God by opening the doorway into God's presence. It begins by establishing the relationship that is needed to open the door. You need to know who *your* Shepherd is to knock on the right door. If you can claim the Good Shepherd as your ultimate source of meaning, then halfway through the psalm the most astonishing thing happens. The door opens.

The God we claim as our shepherd leads us to green pastures that truly nourish us and leads us beside the still waters that cool and refresh us without danger. God leads us in the paths of righteousness, because that is God's nature. We don't want to stray from this relationship, because it reveals who God is, which in turn reveals our own best self, created in God's image. We already know this at a deep level by intuition, so the words of this psalm often break through the crust of our cultural knowing to evoke what we have known since childhood but have "forgotten" as adults.

The door opens when the psalmist shifts ground and begins speaking directly *to God* and we follow. In the words of the King James Bible, we can declare together: "Yea though I walk through the valley of the shadow death, I will fear no evil: for thou art with me; thy rod and thy staff they comfort me. Thou preparest a table before me in the presence of mine enemies: thou anointest my head with oil; my cup runneth over. Surely goodness and mercy shall follow me all the days of my life: and I will dwell in the house of the Lord forever." The result of this relationship is a life that leaves a trail of "goodness and mercy" in its path and provides an eternal dwelling place.

If you learn the Twenty-Third Psalm by heart and can say it out loud to yourself, you will discover the unique quality of this translation's poetry. It was intended to be spoken out loud rather than read silently. In addition to the ringing sounds and measured cadence of the words, this version emphasizes the personal relationship within which we know God. It does this by the pronouns it uses. The archaic "thee" and "thou" call attention to the profound intimacy of being with God.

If you say this psalm to yourself each day, especially out loud, it will change you and your family, even if no one knows what you are doing. It will, as it says, "restoreth your soul," which in turn will spread through the relationships in your family to help meet the challenges that arise.

A few examples from the Hebrew and Christian scriptures will suggest the long and rich tradition of stories about sheep and shepherds evoking God in addition to the Twenty-Third Psalm. "See, the Lord God comes with might, and his arm rules for him . . . He will feed his flock like a shepherd; he will gather the lambs in his arms, and carry them in his bosom, and gently lead the mother sheep" (Isaiah 40:10–11).

The reality of false, human shepherds—whether commoners or kings— caused the prophets to cry out on behalf of God. Jeremiah said, "Woe to the shepherds who destroy and scatter the sheep of my pasture! . . . Then I myself will gather the remnant of my flock out of all the lands where I have driven them, and I will bring them back to their fold, and they shall be fruitful and multiply. I will raise up shepherds over them who will shepherd them, and they shall not fear any longer, or be dismayed, nor shall any be missing, says the Lord" (Jeremiah 23:1, 3–4).

The whole of Ezekiel 34 is about how human shepherds have failed God's flock. It concludes by saying, "For thus says the Lord God: I myself will search for my sheep, and will seek them out. As shepherds seek out their flocks when they are among their scattered sheep, so I will seek out my sheep. I will rescue them from all the places to which they have been scattered on a day of clouds and thick darkness" (Ezekiel 34:11–12).

In the Gospels, John 10 continues this tradition, but now it is *Jesus* who is the Good Shepherd. He calls the sheep by name and leads them to the good grass and still waters. The sheep follow him for they know his voice and he calls them by name. Not only does Jesus lead the sheep, but he will give his own life for them, unlike the shepherd who only watches the sheep for money and not out of love. When the wolf comes, the ordinary shepherd runs away, but the Good Shepherd remains and would die for the sheep.

This great tradition of God as the Good Shepherd is also found in the parable of the lost sheep, which is a companion to the parable about the lost coin.[1] The Good Shepherd searches for the lost sheep (Luke 15:3–7; Matthew 18:10–14) and the Good Housewife searches for the lost coin (Luke 15:8–10). When the lost sheep and coin are found, there is great rejoicing.

John Dominic Crossan noted that the parable shifts the theme of sheep and shepherds so that we become the searchers for God. He wrote, "all of us, male and female alike" become "searchers for what we have lost."[2]

God is the one who cares and who would do anything to lead us to be the kind of sheep who are found and become good shepherds. When the story of God as the ultimate caregiver is combined with the parable that subverts it, making us searchers for God, the meaning shifts to make our relationship with God one of mutual searching and caring. This is a story worth telling to our families.

"Storying" the Good Shepherd

There are times in the lives of families when we need to re-center. We need to pause and ask what is *really* important and how God's caring nature is making itself known in our lives. The need to re-center often occurs in the extremes of death, aloneness, the need for meaning, and the threat of freedom when our ability to create goodness and mercy and leave it in our path is thrown into doubt.

One way to pause and ask what is really important is to say the Twenty-Third Psalm. Another way is to say and do what is described here. As you move the pieces of the story across the green underlay in a meditative way,

---

1. The parables of the lost coin and the lost sheep are short, but the parable of the lost son is much longer (Luke 15:11–32) and makes the theme of losing and finding more complex. In the longer parable the father does not search for his son. The son discovers what he has lost and returns on his own which is not as simple as it first sounds. This parable is often called "The Prodigal Son" and has a life and complexity of its own apart from the lost sheep and the lost coin, but it is worth reading alongside them.

2. John Dominic Crossan, *The Dark Interval: Towards a Theology of Story* (Farmington, MN: Polebridge Press, Eagle Books, 1988), 81–82.

the parable invites us into God's presence and into our own deepest identity to center our family and ourselves.

This material is also available from Godly Play Resources. It includes a green underlay, twelve brown strips, three dark places where the light does not shine, a blue piece of felt for water, five sheep, and two standing figures. One figure is the Ordinary Shepherd and the other is the Good Shepherd. The green spot on the gold box identifies the parable by using color and texture to identify it instead of introducing a pre-existing interpretation by naming it. This allows the parable to speak for itself as much as possible, despite our understandable need to give it a name, as I have done. The story

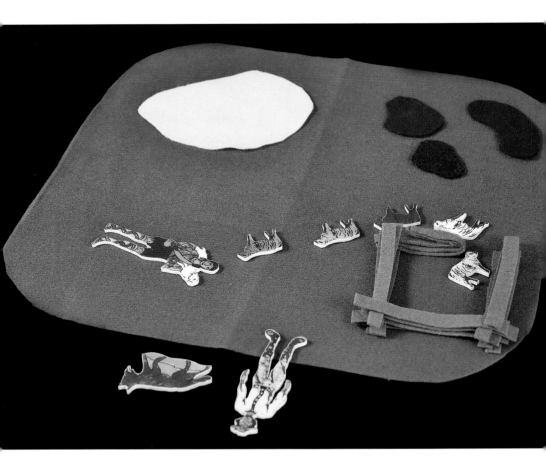

establishes the world of the parable, and then its parabolic nature questions that world to pull us in two directions: God seeks us, as we seek God. Both searches are going on at the same time when we "story" the Good Shepherd and live it in our lives.

This presentation begins by wondering about the gold box. This helps begin wondering about how our journey into God's nature and our own deep identity might evolve. You then remove the lid and take out the things in the box to "build" the world of the parable on the underlay. Next, you tell the parable and wonder together about what the different parts of the parable might *really* be. Finally, you put everything back into the box and replace the lid to conclude.

What to Do and What to Say

MOVEMENTS	WORDS
Pick up the box. Look at it with appreciation and curiosity.	I wonder what this could be? It is gold, so maybe there is something important inside.
Turn the box this way and that, as you wonder about it. Set it down between you and the people you are presenting it to.	It could be a parable. Parables are important. Their words are like gold.
Pick up the box again and hold it out to the others, like a present, as you say:	The box also looks like a present, like something you might give to someone.

Set it down again. Move your hand over the lid to feel the roughness.

It also looks old. Hmm. Parables are old, so maybe there really is a parable inside. Did you know that parables were given to you before you were born? You don't have to do anything to get them. They are already yours.

Tap the lid and trace its dimensions. Pretend to try to open it.

See the lid? Parables are like that. Sometimes they are very hard to open.

Sit back and look at the box.

I have an idea. Let's try to open the box to see what's inside.

Open the box with dramatic "difficulty" and place the box in the lid. Take out the underlay and smooth it out while you say with wonder:

Green. Green. Green. There is nothing here but green.

As you smooth out the underlay, invest it with your respect, wonder, and value. Place the blue piece at your upper left of the underlay.

Here is something blue.

Take out the three black pieces and place them in your far upper right.

Here are some dark places.

Take out the twelve brown pieces of felt and carefully form them into a square, overlapping the pieces at the corners.

I wonder what this could be? Look it is getting stronger.

Point to the inside and outside.

Look. There's an inside and an outside.

Put your finger in the middle of the brown piece farthest from you and pull it up from the right side to make a door. Move it up and down, as you say:

We need a gate so someone inside can go outside and someone outside can come inside. But I wonder who lives there?

Place the five sheep in the sheepfold.

Oh, it's a place for sheep.

Sit back and look at the completed layout for the sheepfold. Pause. Collect yourself, then say:

There was once someone who said such amazing things and did such wonderful things that people just had to ask him who he was.

Take the Good Shepherd out of the box and hold it in your hands to show the figure to the others.

One time when they asked him who he was, he said, "I am the Good Shepherd."

Place the Good Shepherd to the right of the sheepfold, facing the others, and begin to speak for the Good Shepherd.

I know each one of the sheep by name.

Touch each of the sheep, moving your finger along the head and back.

When I take the sheep from the sheepfold, they follow me.

Move the Good Shepherd in front of the sheepfold and then off to your left into the grass at the lower left of the underlay. Move the sheep out of the sheepfold in a line following the Good Shepherd as you say:

I walk in front of the sheep to show them the way.

Smooth the green grass in the lower part of the underlay with the palm of your hand.

I show them the way to the good grass . . .

Move the Good Shepherd toward the water with the sheep following. (You may need to sand the figures with fine sandpaper from time to time so they will slide smoothly over the felt.)

. . . and I lead them beside the cool, still, fresh water.

Move the Good Shepherd around the upper part of the water and turn him toward your right, then stop. Smoothly move the sheep so they come to rest along the upper curve of the water. Turn each one so the head is in the water like they are drinking. Let them drink for a moment before moving on.

Move the Good Shepherd on toward the black felt pieces and then move him through the place of danger, with the sheep following him, as you say:

And when there are places of danger, I show the sheep how to go through.

The sheep move from side to side as they go through to show that they are wary and worried. Tuck the last one under one of the pieces of black felt with only the head showing.

Move the Good Shepherd toward the sheepfold and place him back in his first position. Move the sheep into the sheepfold.

Count the sheep as they go inside by touching each one with your finger.

I count each one of the sheep as they go inside.

Put your finger down on the underlay to show the absent, lost sheep is not there.

If any one of the sheep is missing, I would go anywhere to look for the lost sheep . . . in the grass, by the water, even in places of danger.

Move the Good Shepherd smoothly through the good grass, by the water, and then to the place of danger, as you speak. When the Good Shepherd finds the lost sheep, put it on his back. It goes behind the one already shown on the Shepherd's shoulders. The children won't mind, but adults might.

And when the lost sheep is found, I put it on my back, even if it's heavy, and carry it back safely to the sheepfold.

With one hand move the lost sheep into the sheepfold and with the other hand turn the Good Shepherd around and put him back in the first position, where he began the parable. Close the door, and when all the sheep are safe inside, say:

When all the sheep are safe inside, I am so happy that I can't be happy by myself, so I invite all of my friends and we have a great celebration.

Pause for a moment, then put the Good Shepherd in the box and take out the Ordinary Shepherd. Hold this new figure in your two hands to show it to the others. Place it in the center of the underlay.

This is the Ordinary Shepherd. When the Ordinary Shepherd takes the sheep from the sheepfold, he does not always show the way, so the sheep . . . wander.

Move the sheep out of the sheepfold so one goes to the nearby right and another to the left. Another goes to the far right and the fourth one to the far left. The fifth one goes past the Ordinary Shepherd to the center of the far edge of the underlay.

Take the wolf from the box and show it to the others. Place the wolf by the dangerous place, facing the scattered sheep.

When the wolf comes, the Ordinary Shepherd runs away.

Move the Ordinary Shepherd off the underlay to your near left and place him back in the box.

*Take the Good Shepherd from the box
and place him just beyond the sheepfold
between the wolf and the sheep. Put
him down firmly and leave your hand
on him for a moment to show the
strength of this move.*

But the Good Shepherd stands
between the wolf and the sheep and
would even give his life for the sheep,
so they can come back safely to the
sheepfold.

*Turn the sheep slowly around to face the
sheepfold. Move them slowly back inside.
Put the Good Shepherd back in his first
position, close the gate, and remove the
wolf. Sit back and reflect silently for a
moment about what has happened.*

*Gather yourself to have the quiet energy
and creativity to lead the wondering.
As you wonder, allow the others to have
plenty of time for reflection before going
on. Touch the pieces of the parable as
you wonder about them.*

Now, I wonder if these sheep have
names?

Touch each one.

I wonder if they are happy inside this
place?

Trace the sheepfold.

I wonder where this place could really
be?

*Trace the sheepfold again and open
your hands to gently overshadow the
whole enclosed space.*

I wonder if you have ever come close
to such a place?

Don't look up, even if you are speaking to those gathered. Keep looking where you would like the others to look. In this case your gaze is inviting them to look at the good grass.

I wonder if you have ever found the good grass?

Move your hand smoothly across the lower left of the underlay.

I wonder what the good grass could really be?

Keep looking at the parable.

Touch the "water."

I wonder if you ever tasted the cool, still, fresh water?

Place your hand in the "water."

I wonder if the water ever touched you?

Move your finger through the dangerous place to suggest going through the danger.

I wonder if you ever had to go through a place of danger?

I wonder how you got through?

I wonder if you have ever been lost?

As the wondering begins to slow down, you need to be alert, because you want to end the wondering while there is still some energy left in it.

I wonder if you have ever been found?

Touch the Good Shepherd.

I wonder if the Good Shepherd has ever called your name?

I wonder where this whole place could really be?

*Sweep your hands over the whole
parable laid out on the underlay.*

*When the wondering is over, place the
objects back in the box with great care.
Do not hurry. You do not know what
feelings these pieces have been invested
with during the telling of the parable.
Name the pieces as you put them back
in the box.*

Here are the sheep.
The sheepfold.
The water.
The dangerous places.
The Good Shepherd.

*Be deliberate as you finish the presen-
tation. Dramatize the folding up of the
underlay, especially if there are younger
children present, so they will be able to
do this on their own. You might say for
the younger ones:*

Watch how I fold up the underlay.
I put this side next to the other side.
Look. It makes a new side. I put the
new side next to the old one. Now
take this end and put it next to the
other end. This makes a new end.
I put the new end next to the old one.
Now it will fit in the box.

The Parable of the Good Shepherd can be used for many occasions when
you want to invite God to come and be with you as you search for God in
a serious but playful and creative way. This includes times when we don't
know what to say, like when there is a death, a tragic accident, when a loved
one is in the hospital, or other times. We seldom ask about God's nature
out loud at such times, but we do wonder about it. How could God allow

this to happen? This is an unanswerable question, but it is very authentic and profoundly real. The "answer" is not a concept but a story to be told and responded to.

A constructive response to unanswerable questions about God's nature or motives is to present the parable, as just shown, and trust it to open the door into God's presence. The "answer" is in the creative relationship that evolves, not clever words and arguments. You can trust in this approach. It has been tested. It was first used in children's hospitals in 1974 and continues to be used in such extreme settings to this day. In hospitals the parable is spread out on children's beds or on the floor of the playroom. How the parable works or communicates across cultural barriers, like science and religion or other boundaries, is not obvious at first, so let me tell you a story to show you what I mean.

Christianity as Grounded Openness

I sat on the floor of a Houston Methodist church in the 1990s with a dozen Cambodian children to present the Parable of the Good Shepherd. Their average age was about seven. I was not sure whether they were Christian or not, but Christians had welcomed them as refugees.

The children understood some English, but more importantly they engaged the presentation with their senses, following the pieces of the parable as I moved them smoothly across the green underlay. Their connection with their own deep self, with others in the circle, with God, and with the larger world, past and present, appeared profound as their heads nodded up and down and their eyes widened.

After the presentation we wondered together about what we had experienced together, but they had little to say. This did not seem to be a language difficulty. Their bodies were active, so I wondered if they had gotten in touch with the monstrosity of what they had experienced growing up in the killing fields of Cambodia. That experience was too awful to put into words—in any language.

I showed the children the art materials I had brought to help them go deeper into their existential concerns, which the parable often arouses.

They especially liked the large paintbrushes, the tempera paints in pots, and the big pieces of thick paper. They worked for about thirty minutes as I watched quietly, staying with them on the floor but a little distance away. I tried to radiate my honest but silent support for the tremendous effort of their creativity. I wanted to respect their space but also anchor a safe place as they struggled.

The children's concentration was profound. Most of them painted tigers in a very dark jungle, full of lumpy clumps of black and purple paint. Their paintings were as different as their fingerprints, but they seemed to share a common theme. They needed to make meaning about the danger of dark places. The Parable of the Good Shepherd gave them a means to do this.

Conventional wisdom might argue that what happened was unlikely and my interpretation is too "romantic." The cultural differences were too great for such profound communication to take place and healing to begin. It is true that our backgrounds were quite different. I had grown up in a Presbyterian church in a small farming and ranching community in Western Kansas, where sheep and shepherds were suspect to say the least. The Cambodian children had grown up in Southeast Asia, surrounded by jungle. Their places of worship were shaped by a very different and ancient culture.

The children grew up speaking Cambodian, and the prevailing religion in their country was Theravada Buddhism, practiced by nearly 95 percent of the population. They had probably never even heard of sheep and shepherds, much less met any. Perhaps I should have talked about the relationship between an elephant and its mahout, who rides and takes care of the elephant. That would be more familiar to them. Still, the parable about sheep and shepherds worked well for them and is why I suggest it will work for you and your family.

I think there are seven reasons why it will work. All seven have to do with ways of making meaning that all human beings share. It is likely that a story of God will be able to communicate its depth, despite cultural differences, when it is grounded in our common humanity.

The first commonality is a sensitivity to the *relationships* involved, regardless of what images are used to show them. This is debatable, but the parable's interest in relationships invites participants into this network to connect with it nonverbally. The children knew that I felt these connections, so we shared the parable's openness to the importance of relational depth.

Since the children could relax in the safety of the circle, they could wonder about the relationships in the parable. This allowed them to express the pain they had hidden from themselves and others to create new meaning about it. Their fears overflowed into their paintings, which were respected and accepted. This contributed to the opening of the creative process, which began the process of healing.

A second access to depth in the parable was through the use of movement and touch to tell the story in addition to sight and hearing. Even taste was included among the senses involved, since a simple "feast" of cookies and juice was included in the experience so the children could "taste" the love of the Parable Maker who created the parable and the love by which it was presented to them. Children all over the world learn through their senses, so the knowing of the body was as familiar to the Cambodians as it is to us. They felt at home in that world.

The third way to depth in the parable was through allowing the children's existential limits of aloneness, death, the threat of freedom, and the need for meaning to emerge. These limits to our being and knowing often need to be addressed indirectly, like through the parable and the art response to it, because our existential limits are overwhelming if approached directly. Certainly the storyteller needs to be comfortable with our human limits so there is no unspoken censoring of the telling or hearing of the parable.

The fourth human commonality that opened the way to depth across cultural lines was play. The children recognized the nonverbal signs for play, such as a smile or a twinkle in the eye. When the parable was presented playfully, they shifted easily into this "what-if" mode. They knew instinctually what many of the nonverbal cues for play meant since these signals belong to our common humanity. This is why the children understood the storyteller's invitation.

A fifth depth connection was made through the children's natural spirituality. It is becoming more and more clear to researchers that all children have a special ability to access their spirituality. Dr. Lisa Miller's *The Spiritual Child*, published in 2015, is an example of this research. It was clear in the case of the Cambodian children that they accepted the parable's invitation to engage their spiritual nature in creative ways to cope with their awful experiences, regardless of the pain involved or what adults had inadvertently conveyed to them about repressing it.

The sixth kind of depth connection was love. The children responded to the love of the Parable Maker *who created the parable* and the love *by which it was presented*. This signaled nonverbally the emotional tone of the experience that they were invited into and that held the circle together.

Finally, when the Cambodian children were invited to use the parable to create existential meaning, they recognized that this was an invitation to enter into the deep channel of their own creative process. They felt the safety within the parable's structure and content, as well as the openness by which it was presented. This balance gave them access to their own creativity and that of the Parable Maker, who made the parable. This affinity across the centuries stimulated their own creativity to help renew and re-create their lives.

The experience with the Cambodian children shows how the Parable of the Good Shepherd, presented as described above, can provide spiritual guidance across cultural divides. This means that if this communication from depth to depth was possible for the Cambodian children in an American Christian setting, it may also be possible for your own family.

Conclusion

There are always whispers of divinity in family conversations, but we need to listen carefully to be able to hear them. The Parable of the Good Shepherd is a good way to open up our awareness of God's presence unconfined by our cultural limitations and personal defensiveness. The Good Shepherd does not "explain" God, which is impossible. Instead we are invited to enter into this story of sheep and shepherds to meet God's creative presence in which we can gain a sense of God's care for us as well as our own calling to be good shepherds.

This story of God invites everyone in the family to seek and experience the presence of the Good Shepherd to know God and how to live best according to our own true nature. Many children intuitively steer their lives between rigidity and chaos to be like the Good Shepherd, who creates for others, but we adults need to seek this awareness consciously and guard its significance. We all need to find an appropriate kind of language to reinforce and articulate our awareness of the flow of this reality. The language of the Christian people is such a language.

Christian language, such as the stories of sheep and shepherds and all the stories of God, is the language of love. It needs to be taught with love to affirm and support our deep identity as creators.

In the next chapter we will gather up all the chapters to this point and turn them into a family theology. That sounds a bit formal, but instead of getting abstract we "will story" this by using the circle of the liturgical year to give shape to what we have done so far with stories of God in the home.

CHAPTER 6

The Story of Our Wholeness with God

The Liturgical Circle

of the Church Year

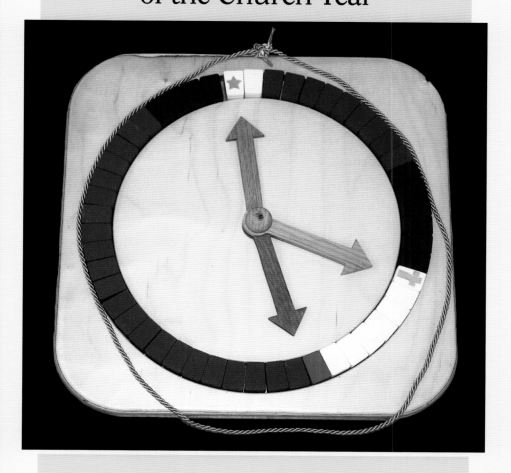

We have now talked about how to present five stories of God at home. They are Creation, Christmas, Easter, Pentecost, and the Good Shepherd. When we put these stories in a circle, their significance as a unified whole appears. The circle represents four important levels of the creative process. First, there is God's circle, which represents God's creative energy flowing out from and returning to God. Our personal circle of the creative process is a second level. It involves wonder, scanning, insight, the development of the insight, and a soft closure. There is also the church's liturgical circle, which if followed with insight and wisdom joins us with God. Finally, there is the circle of our families, as we deal creatively with the perennial challenges of life and death.

Sometimes the church keeps time in a line with a beginning and an ending, but it also keeps liturgical time in a circle, where for every beginning there is an ending and for every ending there is a beginning. This chapter will emphasize the liturgical circle and the circles of our families, but all four circles are always playing back and forth to support each other.

The Center and the Circumference

People have used the circle since prehistoric times to represent the overarching intimations of God. Consider the example of Stonehenge in England. It is a circle made from enormous standing stones, which expressed something about God's creative power and how to participate in it. It has been in existence since about 3,000 BCE.

More recently circles of God appeared in the Bible. Perhaps, the most famous example is Ezekiel's vision from the sixth century BCE. When he was thirty and living among the exiles from Jerusalem by the river Chebar, Ezekiel saw wheels within wheels in a vision. They were made of gleaming beryl, a hexagonal crystal, which comes in many colors such as the green of emeralds. The rims of the circles were full of eyes all the way around (Ezekiel 1:5–19).

In the Greek world, circles were used with other geometrical concepts to measure the earth. Euclid (d. 366 BCE), who lived in Alexandria, defined the circle by its center point and circumference. All points on the circumference are equidistant from the center. The interplay between the center point and the circumference became fascinating to theologians during the Middle Ages to speak of God.

The medieval theologians used Euclid's definition of the circle as the background for saying that when God is the center point, this point is everywhere and the circumference is nowhere. Such playful poetry was, of course, nonsense for those seeking to measure the earth, but it was a good way to say that God does not conform to our ordinary thinking about space and time.

Circles dominated Dante's (1265–1321) great poem about his winding journey through hell, purgatory, and paradise. He circled down into the earth, through its center and then out and up, winding around the mountain of purgatory, and then into the nine spheres of heaven. He wrote in his *Paradiso* (xxix.12) that God is "where every where and every when is focused" (*"dove s'appunta ogni ubi ed ogni quando"*), as if God were the infinite center point of his circular journeys through space and time. Finally, in the abode of God, Dante encountered three equal circles of different colors as his soul aligned with the Holy One.

Some four hundred years later, William Blake (1757–1827), the English mystical poet, wrote enigmatically about God and circles in chapter 3 of his *Jerusalem*: "What is Above is Within . . . the Circumference is Within: Without is formed the Selfish Center, and the Circumference still expands going forward to Eternity." We can move, he thought, through the crust of the self and expand into the timelessness of God.

In the early twentieth century, Yeats wrote in a collection of essays in 1912 called *The Cutting of an Agate*, "If it be true that God is a circle whose centre is everywhere, the saint goes to the centre, the poet and artist to the ring where everything comes round again . . . ." He wrote this in an essay called "In the Serpent's Mouth," which refers to the circle a snake makes when it swallows its own tale.

Yeats contrasted perfection in art at the circumference of the circle with the saint at the center, who seeks perfection in life and lives the still point of the circle's center. The artist and the saint need each other, but God and the God-like person are most evident at the center, which is unable to be contained by the circumference. Yeats thought the wholeness of God's infinity and timelessness are at the center with the saint, but God's presence includes the artist a bit farther away from God at the circumference where we and they are more likely to live but still connected to God.

T.S. Eliot (1888–1965) wrote his *Four Quartets* to search for the "still point" where time and space merge. *Four Quartets* was written toward the end of his poetic career and first published together in 1943. The four meditations have a circular structure and in Burnt Norton, the first meditation, the timeless, still point is sought and found in unmoving Love, which is like the center point of a circle, because it will stay in place rather than slipping, sliding, perishing, and decaying with imprecision beyond it.

When we use the circle of the liturgical year to focus our attention on the creative energy flowing out from and returning to God, we are merely continuing this theological play begun as long ago as 3,000 BCE at Stonehenge. The circle helps us say that God is unlimited by our ordinary limits and infers that we and God are connected in some kind of wholeness like a circle.

"Storying" Our Circle of Wholeness with God

The material for "storying" God's wholeness with us is a circle of wooden blocks. The blocks are different colors to show the different liturgical seasons. They give us a way to literally grasp with our hands the joining of God's circle of creativity with our own.

A more elaborate presentation concerning the church year may be found in *The Complete Guide to Godly Play*.[3] We will use the same material but change the presentation so we can weave it together with our family stories.

The circle is cut into a beautiful piece of wood so that the colored blocks of wood symbolizing the Sundays of the year can be fit into it to show the movement of liturgical time. The material includes a golden cord and arrows, but they are used in the longer, classical presentation, so we will set them to one side. This material is also available from the nonprofit Godly Play Foundation.

---

3. Berryman, *The Complete Guide to Godly Play, Volume 2*, 27–40.

Prepare the circle of the church year by checking the colored blocks to be sure they are all correctly placed. You then put the five story boxes, mentioned above, beside the circle. The circle unifies the five stories of God by laying a plaque from each story against the appropriate blocks in the circle. As the story is told, your family's photos and background stories will be laid next to the appropriate blocks so you can connect your stories with the circle of the liturgical year. With this overview in mind, let's turn now to the presentation itself.

What to Do and What to Say

Movements	Words
Prepare the blocks in the circle and put the circle on the table in front of you before the others arrive.	
When everyone is ready, pick up the circle and look at it with interest. Place it back on the table as you say:	This is the circle of the church year, but it is much more.
Move your finger around the circle clockwise several times, saying:	God's creative energy flows out from and returns to God.
Move your finger around the circle several more times.	This also reminds us about the circle of our own creating.
Point to the top of the circle.	Here is the opening in wonder.
Point to the right side of the circle.	Here is the scanning for something new.
Point to the bottom of the circle.	Here is the insight that discovers what is new.
Point to the left side of the circle.	Here is the developing of the discovery.
Point to the top of the circle again.	Here is where the soft closure is made that is ready to open again in wonder.

*Move your finger around the circle
again but pause at the blocks for
Christmas, Easter, and Pentecost.
You don't say anything about them, yet.*

*Move your finger around again and this
time stop a little longer at the three great
liturgical celebrations as you say:*

Here are the three great celebrations
of the church year.

*Point to the Christmas block, the Easter
block, and the Pentecost block as you
name them.*

Here is Christmas. Here is Easter.
Here is Pentecost.

*Point to the periods for getting ready for
the three great times.*

Here are the times for getting ready.

*Move your finger along the blocks, as
you say:*

This is the time for getting ready to
enter the mystery of Christmas. It is
called Advent.

This is the time for getting ready to
enter the mystery of Easter. It begins
with Ash Wednesday and is called
Lent.

The time of Easter continues from
Easter to Pentecost. This is called
Eastertide. It also helps us get ready
to enter the mystery of Pentecost.

*Move your finger on around the circle
to show the long season of Pentecost.*

After Pentecost Sunday the year continues with the season of Pentecost
until the circle ends to begin again
with the first Sunday in Advent.

Pause again and then point to the center. Move your finger around the whole circle again as you talk about creation.

God is the center extending to infinity, so the center includes the three great times that help connect us with God.

Pause. Look at and touch each of the five boxes that you already placed in a line close to you.

The stories of God are in these boxes. You already know each one, but the circle of the church year will show us how they are connected.

Pick up the box for the Good Shepherd.

Here is the Good Shepherd caring for us and showing us how to care for each other.

Open the lid and take out the pieces including the underlay and place them in the center of the circle.

God is the source and home for all we seek.

Replace the lid on the box and move it to one side.

Pick up the box with the Creation story in it.

Here is the Creation.

Put it back on the table. Open the box and take out the sixth plaque. Show it to the others, then lean it on the blocks at the top of the circle, facing the others.

On the seventh day God gave us a day to rest and remember all the days of creation.

Replace the lid, and move the box to one side.

Pick up the Christmas box. Place it back on the table and open it.

Here is Christmas.

Take out the plaque for Christmas Day and lean it against the blocks for Christmas as you say:

In the mystery of Christmas, we find unending wonder.

Replace the lid, and move the box to one side.

Pick up the box with the Easter things inside. Place it back on the table.

Here is Easter.

Take out the last card and show it to the others. Lean it against the wooden blocks that represent Easter.

On this side we see the one who was crucified. On the other side we see the one who is still with us, and you cannot pull them apart. That is the mystery of Easter.

Replace the lid, and move the box to one side.

Pick up the box with the Pentecost things inside. Place it back on the table.

Here is Pentecost.

Take out the final plaque, showing Pentecost. Lean it against the block that shows Pentecost Sunday.

This is the time when the Holy Spirit awoke Jesus' followers to make them leaders to love and care for others as well as themselves.

Replace the lid, and move the box to one side.

Pause and look at the circle. Touch God in the center, the Creation, Christmas, Easter, and Pentecost.

Move your finger around the circle again.

This is also the circle of our family.

Sit back and look at the circle. Trace the whole circle again with your finger.

Now, I wonder where our family is in this circle? Let's put some family pictures around it to see how they are part of the stories of God.

Bring out your box of family pictures, going back for as many generations as you can find. Place the box on the table. As you open it, say:

I wonder how many stories you know about our family?

Look through the box of pictures and select a few to tell their stories.

I wonder how each story is like a story of God?

Touch the stories of God and then touch the many photographs.

Pick up each of the pictures and ask the group where it should go. Should it be placed by Christmas, Easter, Pentecost, or by Creation at the top of the circle? Should it go at the center where the Good Shepherd is?

I wonder where we should place this picture? Does it go here? Here? Here?

Sort through the family pictures. Tell the stories they represent. Talk about how they link to the stories of God as you place each one by a God story.

When all the pictures have been placed or people begin to lose interest, lift your hands over the whole circle, now covered with its collection of pictures, and say:

I wonder where our family really came from? I wonder where we are now? I wonder where we are going?

Pause for a moment as you reflect on this. Support the conversation about your family's past, present, and future. When the conversation begins to lose its energy, sweep your hand over the whole circle and the photographs. Look at those gathered and say:

What shall we do with all this?

Pause and allow all who wish to speak. Then shrug your shoulders and say:

I guess all we can really do is give thanks! We can give thanks to God for all of us here and for those who came before and all those who will come after us. Thanks be to God!

Amen.

Leave the things on the table for those gathered to wonder about and to continue looking at as they wish. Come back later to put everything away.

This story of God takes a little more time and, perhaps, patience to celebrate. You will need to find and gather your family pictures, which is something we usually mean to do but never quite get around to getting done. It is a good idea to make copies of the pictures to create a special set to keep with this presentation. You also need to find an intriguing box that is just right to put your photographs in. This story of God is worth the extra trouble, because it weaves together the rich visual resource of family stories with the circle of God's stories. This will provide sustenance for the present and enlarge your reservoir of meaning to meet future challenges.

Integrating God with God's Image

What does it mean to integrate God with God's image to make us whole? The movement of creative energy moving out from and returning to God is our natural home. We live in an invisible river of energy, but we need to find the deepest, most life-giving part of the river, so we can be in it and it can flow through us to make us creatively one with the movement of the river. We are in the river while the river is in us.

John had something to say about this in his Gospel. He may have been present in the upper room on that Thursday night long ago. After Jesus and the disciples shared the bread and wine, Jesus quietly washed the disciples' feet. It was clear that his spirit was troubled. He asked, "Do you not believe that I am in the Father and the Father is in me? The words that I say to you I do not speak on my own; but the Father who dwells in me does his works. Believe me that I am in the Father and the Father is in me; but if you do not, then believe me because of the works themselves" (John 14:10–11). He knew that his disciples, those who had come so far with him, still did not understand what was going on. It must have been disheartening.

Jesus continued, "In a little while the world will no longer see me, but you will see me," which must have alarmed them. It also showed that Jesus was speaking with as much faith and hope as love. He then said, ". . . because I live, you also will live. On that day you will know that I am in my Father, and you in me, and I in you" (John 14:19–20).

Jesus then told the disciples how he was like "the true vine." He extended this saying to tell them, "I am the vine, you are the branches. Those who abide in me and I in them bear much fruit, because apart from me you can do nothing" (John 15:5).

Jesus continued talking with them as they sat around the table. At one point he said, "I have said these things to you so that my joy may be in you, and that your joy may be complete" (John 15:11). They must have thought, "This doesn't sound very joyful," but their view of joy may have been limited to happiness. Jesus already understood the joy of Easter. It was equal parts sorrow and happiness. Then he said, "A little while, and you will no longer see me, and again a little while, and you will see me" (John 16:16). Now they were confused as well as worried.

Finally, Jesus looked up into the heavens and prayed for them. His hour had come, so he spoke to God. As he prayed, he said, "I in them and you in me, that they may become completely one, so that the world may know that you have sent me and have loved them even as you have loved me" (John 17:23). They must have felt Jesus' blessing resting on them but there was still urgency in his voice that they did not yet understand.

After Jesus had spoken and prayed, he led the disciples out of the upper room through the dark streets of Jerusalem. They went across the Kidron Valley to the hills on the other side where there was a garden. The Temple soldiers were there with lanterns and torches. Jesus went up to them and asked whom they were seeking. They said, "Jesus of Nazareth." Jesus replied, "I am he," perhaps speaking this ultimate I-Am statement slowly and thoughtfully. The long night and day began that ended in his crucifixion and Easter morning.

The logic of I-in-You-and-You-in-me has been passed down to us from that Thursday evening in Jerusalem. Someone who picked up this theme was William Blake (1757–1827), whom we have already mentioned. He wrote at the beginning of his *Jerusalem*:

This theme calls me in sleep night after night, and ev'ry morn
Awakes me at sunrise; then I see the Saviour over me
Spreading His beams of love, and dictating the words of this mild song:
"Awake! Awake! O sleeper of the Land of Shadows, wake! expand!
I am in you, and you in Me, mutual in Love Divine;
Fibres of love from man to man thro' Albion's pleasant land."

I hope you can forgive Blake's "man to man" and "Albion's pleasant land," but please read instead something like "from one to another in this world round." I suspect, if pressed, he would agree to this change, despite its awkward poetic cadence, because when anyone, woman or man, steers into the deep channel of the great river of creative energy flowing out from and returning to God they become "mutual in Love Divine."

What I am saying is that we were all prepared at the beginning of time and at our own births for a particular kind of wholeness that involves the image of God within us. Our deep identity as creators begins with the wonder of the infant. At first we absorb the world around us through the openness of wonder, but as those who care for us withdraw a bit, we begin to realize that they are independent of us. This requires us to create a world beyond ourselves, which in turn creates the outer and inner worlds we participate in. This act of creating (learning) creates the creative process by which we create knowledge of the world around and within us.

The creation of the creative process involves the whole child, since we cannot yet make fine distinctions about the world beyond us or ourselves without language. This is why our original awareness is unitive. As childhood progresses, however, the wholeness of our fundamental, absorbing wonder, which includes both God and ourselves, begins to differentiate into knowledge of the inner and outer worlds.

As we gain language and become more articulate, the five steps of the creative process by which we do our knowing become differentiated into the four fundamental dimensions of our being. Each dimension develops its own vocabulary and seemingly independent function. In some people these four dimensions—flow, play, love, and contemplation—become integrated over the decades without confusing them. In this integrated state they reveal our true nature as creatures who create, as the Hebrew sages spoke so poetically about long ago in Genesis.

The four dimensions of the creative process share the same characteristics. We can see this by looking at classical definitions of each dimension's process. For example, Mihaly Csikszentmihalyi defined the characteristics of creative flow with much the same structure as others attributed to play such as Johan Huizinga and Brian Sutton-Smith. This structure is similarly found in Paul's classic definition of love (1 Corinthians 13) and in the definition of contemplation by Richard of St. Victor in twelfth-century Paris. When we consider these classical definitions of flow, play, love, and contemplation together, the similarity of the characteristics become evident. Since they come from the same source we are provided with a rich definition of our deepest nature.

Conclusion

This book intends to evoke the wholeness that connects you and your family with God. This chapter draws together a theology for you and your family to live by. This may sound a bit grand, as we already said, but it is true, even if it takes some thinking about. May God be in you as you are in God.

This brings us to the next chapter. It is quite different from those that have gone before it. It gathers together stories *about the stories* of God. Sometimes these stories can lead into the stories of God and sometimes the stories of God lead into them. You are invited to add to this collection to make your own library of stories about the stories of God.

CHAPTER 7

Stories about the
Stories of God

We have talked about six stories of God. There are many more, to be sure, but these six are fundamental. Now let's lay them beside another kind of story so the interplay can illuminate both. Let's pair our stories of God with classic children's books, recognizing that such books are not just for children.

It is a lot to ask to read stories out loud with your family, but there is a lot to gain. Reading and discussing the interplay between the stories of God and "children's" stories creates a situation that invites your family to talk about the similar themes in the two kinds of stories to better understand your own story.

Reading books face-to-face with your family may sound too time consuming until we realize how much time we spend on devices talking to absent and digitized people. We have already talked about the importance of telling family stories face-to-face. Now it is time to talk with Sherry Turkle about the use of screens. In 2015 she published *Reclaiming Conversation: The Power of Talk in a Digital Age.*

Sherry Turkle has spent the last thirty years studying the psychology of people's relationship with technology. She is professor of the Social Studies of Science and Technology at MIT. But why do we need to talk about this? Dr. Turkle answered by saying: "Research shows that those who use social media the most have difficulty reading human emotions, including their own." This is important information for our families and it is cause for concern, but it is not a call to be negative. That is the beauty of having Turkle as our guide. She is not negative and wrote that there is cause for optimism. "We are resilient. Face-to-face conversation leads to greater self-esteem and an improved ability to deal with others." Her watch word is: *"conversation cures."*[1]

Reading out loud with your family takes no preparation, but pays large dividends. It will deepen the meaning and resiliency of your family and help improve empathy and self-esteem to meet future challenges. It is good to begin this custom early so it will seem normal to your children (and to you), so during elementary school, as your children begin to think of

1. Sherry Turkle, *Reclaiming Conversation: The Power of Talk in a Digital Age* (New York: Penguin Books, 2015), 25.

this practice as not only a waste of time but also childish, the practice will already be established and your reading together may have already done a great deal of constructive work to prove itself by that time.

The six children's books I suggest engage significant themes shared with our six stories of God. First, there is the theme of home and a sense of place in *The Wind in the Willows*. This fits with Creation.[2] The second theme is the opening of wonder, as expressed in *Frederick*. It is related to Christmas.[3] Third, there is the redemptive love found in Easter that is beautifully portrayed in *Charlotte's Web*.[4] The fourth theme is our deep identity, which is found in *The Velveteen Rabbit* and is related to Pentecost.[5] The fifth story connects with the themes of generosity and caring evoked by the Good Shepherd. This is related to *A Christmas Carol*.[6] Finally, there is the theme of balanced wholeness with God that is conncected to the liturgical circle of the year. This is found in *The Clown of God*.[7] Let's take a brief look at each one of these books to give you an idea about how they connect to the stories of God and your family stories. They might also inspire you to begin your own family's library of special books to read on a regular basis or on special occasions.

Home and a Sense of Place (Creation): *The Wind in the Willows*

Kenneth Grahame's *The Wind in the Willows* (1908) portrays the kindness and loyalty of friends in a "family" of creatures, unrelated by birth. Each of these different kinds of animals accepts each other's unique idiosyncrasies, as they care for and help each other.

Two kinds of "home" are evoked. One kind is found vividly in a chapter called *"Dulce Domum"* (Sweet Home). The other sense of home expressed

---

2. Kenneth Grahame, *The Wind in the Willows* (New York: St. Martin's Griffin, 1994).

3. Leo Lionni, *Frederick* (New York: Dragonfly Books, 1967).

4. E.B. White, *Charlotte's Web* (New York: Harper Trophy, 1952).

5. Margery Williams, *The Velveteen Rabbit* (New York: Barnes and Noble, 1996).

6. Charles Dickens, *A Christmas Carol* (Greenwood, WI: Suzeteo Enterprises, 2015).

7. Tomie dePaola, *The Clown of God* (New York: Voyager Books, Harcourt Brace and Co., 1978).

is being at home in God's creation, which is treated in the chapter "The Piper at the Gates of Dawn."

Mole and Ratty were on their way home on a snowy evening with thoughts of supper and a fire. Suddenly Mole was overwhelmed with the scent of his old home, where he lived before he came to live with Ratty:

> He stopped dead in his tracks, his nose searching . . . A moment, and he had caught it again; and with it this time came recollection in fullest flood. . . . Home! . . . the home he had made for himself, the home he had been so happy to get back to . . . the home had been happy with him, too. . . .[8]

Mole and Ratty spent the night in Mole's old home. Mole climbed into bed.

> But ere he closed his eyes he let them wander round his old room, mellow in the glow of the firelight that played or rested on familiar and friendly things which had long been unconsciously a part of him, and now smilingly received him back, without rancour.[9]

We all need a place to call home. We need a safe place to venture out from and return to that we can count on. We adults may steel ourselves to living in many places, none of which is completely home, so we lose our ability to be "at home." The energy we invest in each way station to make it feel something like home for us and our children is important, but this assumes that we have an original home to guide us. Without that home place we are set adrift and have trouble finding the home we need as adults as well as children. Mole never forgot his first home, so he knew what home was like when he and Ratty created a home for the two of them.

We speak of "home sickness" when we miss a familiar place and trusted people, but a home can be made with trusted people from outside the family as well as kin, like with the animals in *The Wind in the Willows*. We all need grandmothers, grandfathers, aunts, uncles, cousins, and friends, if they are available, but if they are not available, we need to create a home

---

8. Grahame, 99.
9. Grahame, 116.

with trusted people on our own. We might meet them at church or in some other group. We need wise surrogates for kin, who may be absent or inappropriate, to help with the struggles and to celebrate the pleasures of family life. Trusted friends, who are older and from outside the family, have an authority different from a parent's, which is sometimes needed in families.

The second kind of "home" evoked in *The Wind in the Willows* is the larger home we find in nature. Ratty and Mole were rowing down the river to look for Portly, the lost child of their friend the Otter. They knew he was a wandering child, but he had been missing for too long and his father was worried.

In the early dawn they heard the "glad piping" of panpipes. Rat whispered something about his "song-dream" and a "holy place." Mole too "felt a great Awe fall upon him." They knew an august presence was "very, very near." As they drew closer, the sound became "hushed," but "the call and the summons seemed still dominant and imperious."

When they raised their eyes, their breath stopped, for they were looking into the presence they had felt. It was Pan out of Greek mythology and between his hooves they saw the baby otter, quite at home. Pan was the spirit of the wild places, of shepherds, who often played panpipes, and of flocks. This experience of Pan was the gift of the Creator in the form a "kindly demigod," whose presence was revealed to Mole and Ratty because of their helping and religious natures.

Little Portly woke up and ran about searching for something he sensed he had lost. It was the presence he had been resting in. When he could not find it, he cried bitterly. Mole and Ratty comforted him with understanding and took him home.

When the friends reflected on what happened, they realized that the terror and beauty of the moment had largely been lost. They were disappointed but they both knew that something important had happened, despite their inability to fully recapture it in words.

The warmth and wonder of being at home in God's creation and in your own home was beautifully expressed in *The Wind in the Willows*. This leads us naturally into the wonder of Christmas.

The Sense of Wonder
(Christmas): *Frederick*

Any birth from babies to volcanoes provokes wonder. Something appears where before there was nothing. We ask, "How can our world include such fearful beauty and power?" To answer this question we begin to scan the horizon to enlarge our world to include what has happened. When we arrive at an insight that incorporates the event into our expanded worldview, we go on to create an enlarged vision of our world that includes it. We eventually make a soft closure around this new vision that awaits something wonderful to open the process anew.

Not everyone can or will slow down to appreciate the birth of what is new. Even fewer can express the wonder that occurs when that happens. The celebration of Christmas with all of its ceremony and music attempts to renew the wonder of God's birth. This is like when Frederick recreated the sun's rays and colors of summer in the dark of winter and spoke with his family in a way that gave birth to meaning and energy for them when they were depleted.

Frederick had absorbed the wonder of creation, as the rest of his family went about the very practical and necessary tasks of preparing for winter. While they gathered food, he was intent on gathering experiences to help his family not only survive but thrive during the lean winter months. He wanted to be able to express beauty and power to stimulate their wonder, which in turn would set the creative process in motion for spiritual nourishment and the solving of practical problems. Leo Lionni does that for us in his book *Frederick*, as Frederick did for his family in the story.

Frederick was part of "a chatty family of field mice," who lived well when they were not too far from a farm's full granary. Life was good until the farmers moved away and the barn was abandoned. The granary stood empty. Since winter was coming the mice began to gather food. They all worked at this task day and night except for Frederick.

"Frederick, why don't you work?" they asked. "I do work," he said. "I gather sun rays for the cold dark winter days." He also gathered words to speak when his family ran out of things to chat about and were faced with the question of what their dark days meant.

It began to snow. The field mice retreated into their home in the stones of a wall. They survived well for many months and chatted without thought, telling "stories of foolish foxes and silly cats. They were a happy family," but the food ran out and the stones grew cold. They no longer felt like chatting. That was when they asked Frederick for the "supplies" he had collected. They "remembered what Frederick had said about sun rays and colors and words."

He "climbed on a big stone" and began to talk. They could feel the golden glow of the sun and felt warmer as he spoke. Was it Frederick's voice, his words, or the magic of the moment? They also wanted to see the colors of summer, so Frederick put them into words so they could be felt. He gave his family meaning to make their winter warm.

This is what happens when we experience anew the birth and warmth of Christmas. The poets, like Frederick, have helped us feel the miracle of God's birth and how that flows on into Easter and Pentecost. The wonder of Christmas opens the creative process to discover our deep identity as we begin to move through the circle of the liturgical year, which brings us to Easter and *Charlotte's Web*.

Re-Creative
Love (Easter):
Charlotte's Web

E.B. White (1899–1985) worked for *The New Yorker* among other magazines, but he is best known for publishing three extraordinary children's books: *Stuart Little* (1945), *Charlotte's Web* (1952), and *The Trumpet of the Swan* (1973). *Charlotte's Web* beautifully expresses redemptive love and other Easter themes such as self-giving.

Wilbur was a runt pig. His owner thought he wasn't worth feeding, so he was going to kill him with an ax when the farmer's daughter, Fern, saved him by talking to her father. Later Wilber realized that the farmer was now fattening him up to be killed in the winter. This time Charlotte saved him.

Charlotte was a spider in the barnyard "about the size of a gumdrop." She befriended Wilber and used her energy and creativity to make him *wonderful* so people would feel creative rather than destructive. She wove words of praise into her web like "Some Pig," "Radiant," and "Humble."

With some honest reluctance about thinking of himself as wonderful, Wilber became wonderful and that saved his life.

Charlotte gave much of her own life to save Wilber and to give birth to her own children. This story is about living life richly within our existential limits of death, aloneness, the threat of freedom, and the need for meaning.[10]

"Why did you do all this for me," Wilber asked. Charlotte responded, "You have been my friend." She went on to say, "I wove my webs for you because I liked you. After all, what's a life, anyway?" She then said, "By helping you perhaps I was trying to lift up my life a trifle. Heaven knows anyone's life can stand a little of that."

Wilber guarded her egg sac after Charlotte died and took it back to the barn. When the baby spiders came out of the egg sac, they made little balloons and sailed out the door, but three of the smallest spiders remained with him. Many generations followed to keep Wilber company, as Charlotte had once done.

Charlotte was always very frank about the limits of our existence and her deep friendship with Wilber. Wilber for his part had the capacity to be grateful for her sacrifices and friendship. He understood how important having really good friends can be in times of loneliness and trouble.

Children especially need the honest and frank caring and love that Charlotte showed to Wilber. They will cope courageously and creatively with any situation when they sense that we are deeply and creatively involved in the trouble with them. A synergy develops, so the total energy involved in the family expands rather than contracts. I know this is easier said than done, but if you step back and wonder together about the challenge confronting you, the creative process can begin to work in and among you so the family can "get creative."

I mention this because creativity is not just a strategy. It is who we are. When we recognize and use our deep identity as creatures who create,

10. The four existential limits to our being and knowing were mentioned earlier in this book. They are all touched on in *Charlotte's Web* and other children's books. In *Charlotte's Web* you can see them acknowledged on the following pages among others: Wilber's death 3, 40, 49, 50, 62; Charlotte's death 115, 117, 136; aloneness 27, 31; the need for meaning 164; freedom 17, 19. Charlotte's redemptive, self-sacrificing love can be seen especially at 146, 153, 157, 163, 164, 165, 191.

then we become real. With this in mind let's look next at a story about becoming real.

Becoming Real
(Pentecost):
The Velveteen Rabbit

One day in the nursery the Velveteen Rabbit asked the old Skin Horse about becoming real. This took place in *The Velveteen Rabbit* (1922) by Margery Williams (1881–1944).

"What is REAL?" asked the Rabbit . . .

> "Real isn't how you are made," said the Skin Horse. "It's a thing that happens to you. When a child loves you for a long, long time, not just to play with, but REALLY loves you, then you become Real."
>
> "Does it hurt?" asked the Rabbit.
>
> "Sometimes," said the Skin Horse, for he was always truthful, "When you are Real you don't mind being hurt."
>
> "Does it happen all at once, like being wound up," he asked, "or bit by bit."
>
> "It doesn't happen all at once," said the Skin Horse. "You become. It takes a long time. That's why it doesn't often happen to people who break easily, or have sharp edges, or who have to be carefully kept. Generally, by the time you are Real, most of your hair has been loved off, and your eyes drop out and you get loose in the joints and very shabby. But these things don't matter at all, because once you are Real you can't be ugly, except to people who don't understand."[11]

From Carlo Collodi's *The Adventures of Pinocchio* to *The Velveteen Rabbit*, children's books have been interested in how children and adults become real. It takes time for us to season so our thoughts, words, and actions fit together. This takes a long time, because we are usually scattered and lack a clear understanding of our deep identity so we have trouble living it as a whole. When *we become* our deep identity as creators, we become real.

---

11. Williams, 5.

Children seem to intuit naturally how to seek out and live in the deep channel of the creative process, which is our home, but this is more difficult for adults. We need to work out consciously who we truly are so that can shine through in a consistent way during the living of our days. There is much to distract us and lead us astray. This is why adults "who break easily, or have sharp edges, or who have to be carefully kept" seldom achieve the integration of their deep identity as creators with the Creator to live with integrity.

One summer evening the Velveteen Rabbit discovered that the old Skin Horse was right about becoming real. The Rabbit had been left outside. The Boy, who was recovering from Scarlet Fever, couldn't go to sleep without him, so Nana went out into the yard to get the old Bunny. When she returned with him she said casually and mostly to herself, "Fancy all that fuss for a toy." The little Boy was suddenly alert. He sat up in bed and said, "Give me my Bunny!" He then firmly proclaimed, "You mustn't say that. He isn't a toy. He's REAL!"[12]

When the Boy recovered, the doctor ordered the old Bunny to be thrown out to be burned with other things that had been infected. This was when the old Bunny discovered a whole new kind of reality. The discovery came while he was in near despair about being thrown away. He said to himself, "'Of what use was it to be loved and lose one's beauty and become Real if it all ended like this?' And a tear, a real tear, trickled down his little shabby velvet nose and fell to the ground."[13]

A flower appeared where the tear soaked into the earth. The Fairy of nursery magic came out of the flower and kissed the old Bunny, who then returned to watching some wild rabbits nearby. Suddenly his nose itched and without thinking he scratched it with one of his hind legs.

The Velveteen Rabbit become real in an even larger way than he already was. This was like when we die and become real in a larger way by flowing naturally and completely into the deep part of the creative process that flows out from and returns to God with caring and generosity. This reality brings us to the Good Shepherd, who helps that happen.

---

12. Williams, 11.
13. Williams, 27.

Caring and Generosity
(The Good Shepherd):
A Christmas Carol

The Good Shepherd leads us to grass that is good for us and to water that is quietly thirst quenching rather than turbulently dangerous. He leads us in paths of righteousness that are as natural as being called by the right name. He also shows us how to go through places of danger so we can lead others and our own children in the same way. The Good Shepherd gives his life for the sheep out of loving generosity, which reveals God's nature. We need this revelation to know how to be like God so we can live connected to God through God's image within us, rather than being distracted by the many inadequate shepherds and identities that compete for our attention.

Let's return again to Charles Dickens's *A Christmas Carol* (1843) and lay it alongside the Good Shepherd to discuss this further. We begin with "a squeezing, wrenching, grasping, scraping, clutching, covetous, old sinner." He was screwed so tightly into the rigid, dead wood of his solitary, lifeless routine that it seemed impossible that he could ever be other than he was.

You already know the story and we have already referred to it when we talked about "storying" Easter. The ghost of Scrooge's former business partner, Jacob Marley, now dead these seven years, dragged his chains up the stairs and through the door into Scrooge's bedroom. He forced Scrooge to confront and contemplate his past, present, and future. He knew from experience that otherwise there was no release from the chains Scrooge was forging for himself. Marley had already changed. He cared enough about his old partner to generously trouble his sleep and shock his creative process into action to find a better way to live and die.

When Scrooge woke up on Christmas morning, he too had changed. He had been re-created by reflection. Before Marley's visit he was a man who was not aware of others except as irritations or objects to fleece. After Marley's visit he became a man for others who "went to church and walked about the streets" with joy and generosity.

A Christmas Carol is a story of Christian redemption and the nature of God. We intuitively love to celebrate the change in Scrooge, even if we don't usually associate it with God's nature, Easter and redemptive love.

It touches something deep inside of us, and this "something" is our true nature by which we are re-created to be like God.

It is as if the Good Shepherd restored his soul by leading Scrooge back to green pastures, still water, and the paths of righteousness. God guided him back through the dangerous places with the help of Marley's ghost when he was completely lost. The Good Shepherd found him and returned him to the safety of the sheepfold, and gave him a kind of maturity beyond the norm that he hadn't dreamed of since he was a child.

To "Scrooge" or not to "Scrooge" is the question. Will we get stuck like Scrooge did, or will we find our way into the deep channel of the creative process with Marley and the Good Shepherd leading the way to wholeness with God that gives us true balance for the creative living of our days?

Balance and Wholeness (Circle of the Church Year): *The Clown of God*

How can we balance the pull of rigidity and chaos, which fractures us and leads us to our ruin? How can we keep the form and openness of our creativity whole without getting stuck in either?

We need to learn how to balance the Creator of all with the creator within. We need to be able to juggle the many parts of our daily lives creatively and smoothly, rather than dropping any of the many balls we juggle by becoming mechanical or confused. This is why the story of God's juggler comes to mind. It came from an ancient story Tomie dePaola recreated in his book *The Clown of God* (1978).

Many, many years ago in Italy, a boy named Giovanni lived in Sorrento. He had no mother or father, so he had to create a family of his own. He did this by juggling. He juggled alone as a boy and then became part of a traveling show and juggled with increasingly great art. The crowds cheered. It wasn't long before he left the show and went off on his own. His clothes and juggling became even more elegant.

One day he met some of the friars called poor "Little Brothers" and felt at home. He shared his food with them. They said that when he gave happiness to people he also gave glory to God. Giovanni was not so sure, but he traveled on, juggling. If his art was for God as well as himself and others, then so be it.

Finally, as we all must, Giovanni became old, but people didn't like to see an old clown. One day when he dropped the colored balls, the audience laughed with scorn. Giovanni ran away. He washed off his clown face and stopped juggling. He began to beg like he had when he was an orphaned child.

Finally, Giovanni journeyed back to Sorrento and slept in a deserted corner of the church of the "Little Brothers." He was very weary and had lost track of time when he fell asleep. While he slept the enormous stone space filled with people, for that night was none other than the Feast of Christmas. Suddenly he woke up! There was music and a procession. Gifts were brought to the Holy Child.

When everyone was gone, Giovanni remained. The church grew silent again and shadows took over its vast inner space. He moved closer to the statue of the Lady and the Child with great quietness. He thought the child seemed sad, so he told the Lady in the statue that he wished he had a gift for her child. He paused. Well, he did have a gift.

Giovanni opened his bag, put on his old costume, and revived his clown face. He then stood in front of the statue and juggled like he had never juggled before in his life. His heart was pounding and then it stopped. He fell to the floor dead. When the Brothers found him, they made the sign of the cross, "May his soul rest in peace."

Suddenly one of the Brothers saw something that was hard to believe. The Holy Child was smiling and held the golden ball from Giovanni's juggling in his blessed hands. All was now whole.

Conclusion

The interplay between the stories of God and the "children's" stories in this chapter raises questions for you and your family. Are you going to value home like the creatures in *The Wind in the Willows*? Will you find time to wonder and to create meaning with your family like Frederick did with his? Will you honor redemptive love like Charlotte lived, no matter what? Will you become real like the Velveteen Rabbit? Does renewing your acquaintance with Scrooge suggest that knowing God's love and generosity is worth the trouble of reviewing and reconsidering your life and death? Can you weave these stories and the stories of God together with your family stories, like Giovanni did with his juggling, to become whole with each other and with God?

These questions and others invite you to dwell with these stories for a time to let their many connections with you, God, and your family sink in. When you read them to your children, you are also reading them for yourself. The stories of God and these stories about those stories will help your family prepare to creatively meet troubled times, which are bound to come.

In the next and last chapter, we will turn more explicitly to meeting family challenges. We have spent our time together to this point layering in the levels of stories needed to weave the stories of God together with our family stories. In the next chapter we will discuss family challenges more directly and ask the question about how to prepare for them when we don't know what they will be. The next chapter is about what to do when you don't know what to do.

CHAPTER 8

What to Do When You Don't Know What to Do
Being Ready
for Family Challenges

Many decades ago our family experienced an unexpected challenge. Let's use that event to anchor our discussion about how stories of God can help us meet such challenges. We will then discuss the Play Bag, which is a practical way to open one's creativity under pressure and when there is no pressure to reflect on what the creative process feels like so we can find it when we need it. Finally, we will map the deep channel of the creative process that flows out from and returns to God, because finding the deep channel of this great river is what to do when we don't know what to do.

The Story of a Family Challenge

Our second child, Coleen, was born on January 1, 1967. This joyous event was eagerly anticipated. What was not anticipated was that she would be born with the birth defects of spina bifida and hydrocephalus. Coleen was rushed from the hospital where she was born in Plymouth, a town in northern Indiana, to James Whitcomb Riley Hospital in Indianapolis. They had the experience and staff there to care for her.

I held Thea's hand for a long time in the hospital and then kissed her on the forehead to say "Goodbye." She was dazed and heavily sedated. It was almost impossible to leave her, but I had to go with our new little girl to see what could be done for her in Indianapolis. Someone guided me outside to the ambulance. I recall the vehicle was more like a station wagon than an ambulance. It had a fold-down back door. A nurse brought little Coleen outside tucked into a tiny crib, and placed her on the fold-down door. Time stopped. Someone told me she would probably not survive the trip. I baptized her.

This happened when I was thirty. I thought at the time that I was quite mature and had everything under control. Looking back over fifty years, I can see how young and inexperienced I was and I have compassion for that young man and his wife. I remember him doing the best he could for his little family of three, now newly expanded to a tentative four. We had never talked or thought about what to do in a crisis like this. We had never even heard of "spina bifida" before, and "hydrocephalus" was something that happened rarely and always to other people's children.

When little Coleen and I got to Riley, the receiving staff asked if I wanted to treat. Yes. The doctor wanted to know if I understood the dire prognosis. Yes. The business department wanted to know if I could pay. Yes and No. I was a chaplain, teacher, and coach at Culver, a boarding school, which in those days had about 900 high school boys attending. I made just enough money to be disqualified for financial help.

Coleen lay on an examining table. I learned that part of her spinal cord had not developed normally. I looked into the opening in her back and saw where the spinal cord dissolved and then began again. It was as if communication from her brain to the lower part of her body had been severed. The surgeons would soon close her back to prevent infection, but there was still the related problem of hydrocephaly. She had an abnormal accumulation of fluid in her head, which was causing an enlargement of the skull and the compression of her brain. The surgeons would soon put in a one-way shunt, called a Holter valve or Spitz-Holter shunt, to relieve the pressure. Coleen was taken away to the infant intensive care unit.

I went into the hospital chapel to pray for Coleen and our family, but it was a dark, small, windowless space. It felt like a coffin. I could barely breathe and suddenly became nauseous. I bolted out the door into the open air and looked up silently into the blue upon blue sky. I then searched for a place to sit where the grass was green and the water still. I found a place nearby and rested. I was restored; then I went to see the surgeon.

Late that evening I began the journey back home to Northern Indiana. The ambulance felt enormously empty as we drove through the dark. I was emotionally spent and physically exhausted by the time we arrived back at the hospital. I climbed wearily into our car, still parked outside, and drove the few miles back to Culver. I wanted to pick up Coleen's older sister, Alyda, as soon as possible. She was five and staying with friends. I needed to tell her what had happened and take her to see her mom.

Thea was alone, so very alone, in the hospital. I wept as I drove, imagining her still dazed, as when I last saw her. She had already cared for and loved our new little girl within her for nine months.

Alyda and I sat in the living room of our white house across from the school. She was perched on the edge of the couch, looking very small. I sat slumped in a chair across the room, numb and lost in grief. I had now been awake for over twenty-four hours.

I knew I had to tell Alyda what had happened, but I didn't know how. What could I say? Her new little sister was in big trouble and probably would die in a few days. I began to talk, but the words were garbled, hesitant, and confused.

Alyda broke in. She went right to the point. "Is Mommy dead?"

I got up, crossed the room, and sat down by her on the couch. I put my arm around her. "No. Your Mommy is okay." There were tears. "Let's go see her." That's all she wanted to know. I had missed her most urgent need in my confining grief.

As we drove the familiar road back to the hospital, my thinking began to expand a little. I realized that Thea really, really needed to see Alyda as much as Alyda needed to see her. She needed to know that Alyda was fine. This was something she *could* know unlike Coleen's future.

I also needed to see Thea. I needed our sense of "we-ness" to carry on. We were the ones who brought this family into existence and we were the ones who were going to re-create our dreams and lives to find our way forward together again.

As the hours, days, and months passed, we went through the motions of daily living for a long time before our creativity and energy began to flow easily. A sign that we were almost there was when we began to say, when confronting new challenges, "Okay, let's get creative. It'll be fun."

Coleen did not die that week. She is now a wonderful, young woman of just over fifty years. She "walked," swinging along with her brace and crutches from her toddler days until July of 2014 when she had rotator cuff surgery and needed to shift to a power chair. As a teenager she finished high school and then went to art school. She was a painter. Little Alyda became a beautiful dancer (like her mom) and in college she prepared herself for the field of health care. She and Michael now have three girls of their own, who are in their twenties. One of the greatest challenges to our family was the death of Thea from cancer in 2009, but we are still moving forward, so this is not a sad story. It is about gifts and gratitude.

"Speaking Christian," Gifts, and Gratitude

One of the questions this story raises is how Christian language can help meet unexpected family challenges. As I look back, I see the use of four kinds of Christian communication in our family challenge. One was the moments of touching, like when I kissed Thea to say "Goodbye." Another example is when I crossed the room to give Alyda a hug, as she sat on the couch. Christian language is the language of love, which sometimes needs no words, but always needs to be communicated with love.

A second way Christian language helped was when the doctors asked me whether to treat or not. That question pushed me to my existential limit of knowing and being. Moments of ultimate concern like that are times when religious experience and language can make a difference. My "spontaneous" response came out of my Christian identity. I chose life with my whole being, even if I did not know what to do.

My retreat to the chapel to pray was a search for explicit Christian communication and meaning. My fleeing outside into the open was an intuitive search for the God beyond the confinement of the chapel and my own limits. I also intuited a need for the Good Shepherd of the Twenty-Third Psalm, even if it did not occur to me at the time. I later realized that I didn't know how to use Christian language well in a crisis, despite all my time as a child in church and my theological training. Nevertheless, my body knew what to do because of my formative experience.[1]

Finally, there were the moments when I sighed, "Oh, my God," or whispered "God, help me." These were moments of extreme prayer, even if they were uttered more as a reflex. The "reflex" was cultural and secular, but it was also deeply Christian.

Of course, I didn't reflect on such things at the time, but I did notice them. What I realize now about Christian language is that I had learned it as a matter of information, explanation, decision, and how to apply what

---

1. The baptizing of Coleen was such a deeply natural and positive use of explicit "Christian communication and meaning" that I almost forgot to mention it.

the Bible said to life formally by analogy. I knew the Bible, the history of the Church, theology, liturgical practice, the key languages of Hebrew, Greek, and Latin, and I was experienced in pastoral care. What I didn't know was *how to actually use* Christian language to create existential meaning to steer my way into the deep channel of God's creative flow. I was not fully aware of being created to create and how this connected me to God. This meant that I was also not aware of how important it is *to give thanks* to God for the gift of our deep identity that makes us fully human.

Giving thanks is not just being polite. It is the ground of ethics. When we show our children how to give and receive gifts, we are teaching them the fundamental basis for ethical living. This is because the emotional motive for ethics comes from gratitude and expresses itself in generosity.[2] Ethical living flows out from our appreciation and respect for the gift of life, nature, and other people with whom we create life together. We are born to "let justice roll down like waters, and righteousness like an everflowing stream" (Amos 5:24). People who are not grateful and generous lack the fundamental *capacity to be ethical* as they were created to be.

It takes enormous creativity for families to be ethical in any century. This has been true since we wandered the earth in small clans to the times of ancient plagues and wars. The shift from agrarian life to industrialization and modern warfare also challenged families, as do today's electronic screens and other distractions that obscure our true identity. We can still survive these challenges as our forbearers did by listening well to each other and telling stories of God face-to-face, weaving them together with our own stories. This gives us a foundation that enables us to create new ways for our families to flourish amid the challenges of our own time and place.

This brings us to two final questions raised by the story this chapter began with. One is how do we get in touch with the gift of God's image. The other is how to map the flow of the creative process, so we can locate ourselves in it when we are lost.

---

2. For background to this statement, please see "Chapter 3" in Berryman, *Becoming Like a Child*, 144–80.

Getting in Touch with the Gift of God's Image

What we need to do, when we don't know what to do, is get in touch with the gift of God's image. It is one thing to talk about our deep identity. It is another thing to experience it. To experience it with awareness, we need to be able to identify the feeling of the creative process in action. Using a Play Bag can help. Opening your Play Bag helps open your awareness to your true identity when not under pressure and to enable the creative process to begin to work when the pressure of a challenge is intense.

A Play Bag has games, art materials, and stories in it. This is a case where less is more. You only need a few alternatives to play your way into creativity. It is important to keep this simple, because a crisis pushes us hard to move toward chaos or rigidity instead of staying at home in our true nature, where openness and structure are joined.

The Play Bag is also a means to encourage rapport within the family. "Rapport" is a word that identifies relationships that are close and harmonious, where people understand each other's feelings and ideas through open, honest, and empathetic communication. In a crisis there is a tendency to isolate one's self and close down rapport at the very moment when close, open, and harmonious connections are needed to survive creatively.

You only need to put three games in your family's Play Bag. One is Tic-Tac-Toe. You already know how to play it, so all you need is a pencil and some paper or just lines in the dirt. Draw the cross, where the Xs and Os are placed, and play while you are waiting in a doctor's office or visiting a friend in their home when they can't get out. It doesn't take much concentration, so deeper concerns can arise as you talk while playing the game.

Tic-Tac-Toe soon becomes boring, but its virtue is that you take turns. This encourages communication, but your Play Bag also needs a game of checkers to follow up when Tic-Tac-Toe is no longer interesting. The instructions for checkers are usually inside the lid of the box. It takes up more room in your Play Bag because of the board, and it is more complicated than Tic-Tac-Toe, so it takes longer to play and involves some strategy, which arouses more conversation. Checkers also avoids the complexity of chess, which might take too much concentration. Playing checkers for fun can help expand talk about planning and strategy to meet family challenges as well as building rapport.

Electronic games don't work. They dominate the attention of a single player rather than promoting movement and conversation between players. Electronic games block the rapport your family needs to meet a crisis. It is important for everyone in the family to stay in touch electronically with friends and to search out alternatives for planning, but when challenged as a family, it is time to pull together to create a new future as a creative community.

It is true that some electronic games, such as World of Warcraft, involve other players. Players of WoW form themselves into guilds, which are teams of avatars that go on quests together, but joining those electronic players takes you away from the face-to-face relationships *within your family* when your family is on its own quest to meet very real challenges that involve you all.

It is important to notice that WoW and other electronic games are designed to be addictive, so no matter what the family crisis may be, some will be drawn to screens to distract them from creatively meeting the challenge.[3] Addictions are powerful, so patience and perseverance are both needed to invite everyone into the network of family rapport to create a new future for you all.

The third game for your Play Bag is the simplest and yet most complicated. It is a piece of string. You ceremoniously drop it between you and the other player or players. Let it fall into a random shape. Say: "I wonder what that could be," then wait for the conversation to begin. Donald Winnicott (1896–1971), a child psychiatrist, invented the "squiggle game."[4] He was also widely respected for discovering and writing beautifully about the in-between space between the child and the adult caregiver. He thought that this space is the place where creativity and religion are born and heal-

3. To read more about World of Warcraft and the addiction to games, please see Adam Alter, *Irresistible: The Rise of Addictive Technology and the Business of Keeping Us Hooked* (New York: Penguin Press, 2017), 16–19.

4. To read more about the squiggle game, please see D.W. Winnicott, *Therapeutic Consultations in Child Psychiatry* (London: Hogarth Press and the Institute of Psycho-Analysis, 1971). His *Playing and Reality* (London: Tavistock, 1971) provides the context for this technique.

ing occurs in therapy. When the conversation winds down, drop the string again to see if it will start up another conversation. If not, then it has served its usefulness.

Art materials are also important for your Play Bag. Art is a way to express what is going on with your feelings while still staying in control of them. Crayons, colored markers, paper, glue, scissors, and some scraps of yarn and wood are probably more than enough. Crayons are soft and subtle. You can make many shades of color with them, like mixing black and white to make gray and using the primary colors to make all the rest. Markers are hard, sharp, and brightly defined. They don't mix well to make new colors, but they are easy to use and make bold statements.

The use of color and shapes replaces words. Color shows feelings while shapes make images of the logic we might use later with words. Art allows children and adults to communicate their vision of the world indirectly. This is why we need some privacy and safety to express ourselves this way, and we need support because such expression can be scary.

When I say "support," I don't mean praising the art created. What I mean is affirming what the child or adult is expressing rather than interpreting or valuing it. You might say, "That's very blue." "What a wonderful curving line!" "Hmmm. I wonder what that could be." The creator of the art is the one who needs to interpret it to the onlooker, not the other way around. This kind of art is to express honest feelings to get a handle on them. It is not an art class to shape one's technique.

Stories are the third thing you need in your Play Bag, along with games and art materials. Some may not want to play a game or do art. You can say, "That's ok. I don't feel much like making stuff or playing a game either. What about a story? We can read one or make one together."

"Mutual storytelling" was the idea of psychiatrist Richard A. Gardner (1931–2003).[5] First, invite your child or another adult to start a story. Listen carefully for clues about how the storyteller is thinking and feeling. You

---

5. To read more about mutual storytelling, please see Richard A. Gardner, *Story-Telling in Psychotherapy with Children* (Lanham, MD: Jason Aronson, 1993). Gardner wrote 41 books. His mutual story-telling is listed as one of 35 significant events in the history of play therapy.

can then "tell back" a continuation of the story using the same characters in a similar setting. You might broaden the original story or include some resolution to the conflicts to test what direction the other person needs to go. You might ask, "Is your story going in a direction you like?"

If the other person does not want to begin the story, you can say, as Gardner did, "I will start the story and when I point to you, say the first thing that comes to mind. Ok? Here we go. Once upon a time, in a far-away land, there lived a _____." Gardner also asked such questions as, "What was the little girl thinking when _____?" "Why did the father _____?" "Can you tell me what _____ means?"

I understand what he was doing and why, but it is usually better for what we are attempting here to stay in narrative if possible. You can still clarify motives and relationships by the way you continue the story without changing the form of communication to direct questions. This is especially important with adults, who would rather talk *about* stories than create them. Our intent here is to encourage the use of the creative process.

There are some developmental differences between how children and adults tell stories you might want to keep in mind. Children about five years old tell their "stories" in bits and pieces. They are in a pre-narrative stage, so they process and express their talk as episodes, like a handful of loose pearls. This is one reason why young children like to hear stories over and over again. They need you to keep the episodes connected. This is diffi-cult for them to do on their own because they become absorbed by partic-ular events, which causes them to lose track of the overarching narrative.

Sometime between five and seven years, children begin to string their episodes together, like threading pearls on a narrative string to make a necklace. The episodes are linked by time and space to give movement and shape to the story. These early stories remain open and unselfconscious. The revelations of the self in narrative are a matter of indifference to chil-dren this age, but *about* age nine some censoring begins.

Children after ten or twelve still like stories, but their telling is more self-conscious. Despite their awareness of revealing things about them-selves in their storytelling, they sometimes need to tell stories anyway for that very purpose. On the other hand, they sometimes feel childish if they enjoy stories too much. This is partly because they are absorbing the culture's prejudice against narrative in school.

Children are taught in school that "facts" are more important than stories. When children engage stories in school they are often taught to *analyze* them. This assumes that taking stories apart and translating them into "objective" concepts is more important than the story itself. This approach to stories is important and interesting, but it robs them of their power to enrich the intuition of the tellers and listeners, as they make meaning together.

Your Play Bag also needs to have some stories you can read together. I recommend the stories from the last chapter as a good place to start, but you will also have meaningful favorites from your own growing up that need to be included. It is important that you read the stories you choose with feeling and empathy. They need to mean something to you, to mean something to the listener. Children notice how involved you are, even if they don't comment on it.

You will also need some fancy pieces of paper in your Play Bag. You might say, "Would you like to write your own story? Let's begin by just putting down a list of words. We can fill in the rest afterwards."

As children or adults work at their writing or other kinds of play on their own, it is a good idea to have something for you to do, so you aren't just sitting there watching them. You can be supportive but not intrusive as you read one of the books in your Play Bag or jot down a few words or sentences to begin your own story. It is also good to be alert to the children who do not yet write comfortably. They might want you to write down their words or sentences for them to begin a story.

Sometimes it is good to suggest keeping a diary for older children and adults. Diaries can become very important. This is why you might consider putting two blank diary books in your Play Bag for members of the family to choose between. Someone might want to get started at the very moment you suggest that writing in a diary might be fun.

Be patient. Let these simple pastimes invite you, God, and others into the creative process. If you use the Play Bag with good humor, communication in your family will deepen and become more playful, like that of

John Hull and his son who talked theology together about "Mr. Bird" in chapter 5.

Using your Play Bag well is important to arouse the creative process. It is good to know what the creative process feels like in action and to have playful things to do together to help stimulate the creative process when you and your family are challenged. Most importantly, these activities are just plain fun. Why not do them for no reason at all?

To know more about the deep channel of the creative process, let's turn now to the geography of the great river that flows out from and returns to God. A map makes a journey easier and lets you know when you have arrived. Finding your home in the deep channel of God's river is what you need to do first when you don't know what to do to meet a family challenge.

The Great River of God

The Bible often describes God's creative energy as a great river. In the Hebrew Scriptures we read that Amos, the shepherd of Tekoa, prophesied for God in terms of a river: "Take away from me the noise of your songs; I will not listen to the melody of your harps. But let justice roll down like waters, and righteousness like an everflowing stream" (Amos 5:23–24). To live in this great river of justice, we need enormous creativity and integrity, so finding the deep current of the river that flows out from and returns to God is fundamental to our existence.

Isaiah said that when the poor and needy seek water they will find it, because the Lord will "open rivers on the bare heights, and fountains in the midst of the valleys; I will make the wilderness a pool of water, and the dry land springs of water" (Isaiah 41:18). The psalms go on to say that we are planted like trees by streams of water so that we can drink from the river (Psalm 1:3) and that there is a river that makes glad the city of God (Psalm 46:4). The great river is a gift given to all of us.

As the Christian Scriptures come to a close with John's vision, we read, "Then the angel showed me the river of the water of life, bright as crystal, flowing from the throne of God and of the Lamb through the middle of the street of the city" (Revelation 22:1–2). This crystal clear river of flowing creativity enables justice to roll down for all. It is where we find our deepest identity as creators of creating in others and ourselves, which joins us with God.

The flow of the creative process in the shallows next to the banks of the river is not strong, so the weakness of the current allows the creative process to be used for destructive as well as constructive ends. The deep current which flows in the center of the river is where the creative process is used only for constructive purposes. The four dimensions of the creative process—flow, play, love, and contemplation—are integrated there.

Each of the four dimensions of the creative process share five characteristics. The process is done for itself. It is voluntary and involves deep concentration. It alters time and is pleasurable. This shared set of characteristics is one of the reasons why the four dimensions of the creative process appear to have developed from a common origin, which is the openness of the infant to absorb everything around it.

Another reason the four dimensions appear to come from the same source is that they share the same circular process for creating. This begins with opening then moves to scanning. Insight is the third step, which is followed by the development of the insight, and finally soft closure. The closure is soft to enable the process to open again instead of responding rigidly or drifting into chaos.

Each step in the circle of the creative process, which bubbles and swirls like eddies in the river, carries with it a dominating feeling. Wonder signals the opening of the process. Curiosity expresses scanning. Delight erupts when there is insight. During the development step, we feel a sense of careful caring. Finally, a sense of deep satisfaction indicates soft closure.

The farther we get from the center of the river the more we lose touch with our deep identity. If we get tossed up high and dry on the riverbanks, where each bank defines itself in opposition to the other bank, we risk losing a sense of who we truly are. The opposition of the banks prevents their limits from working together to support the creative process flowing between them.

Another way to say this is to realize that when the openness of comedy, tending toward chaos, and tragedy, which tends toward rigidity, become separated the creative process is destroyed. If one becomes stuck in chaos, nothing is serious. Tears and laughter express madness. Getting stuck on the other bank means that the structure of tragedy becomes rigid and everything becomes serious. Tears and laughter express scorn.

In the middle of the river, where comedy and tragedy play together, the sights and sounds are different. There we hear the happy gasps and gurgles of wonder, the deep chuckle of delight and discovery, and the smooth, flowing smile of satisfaction that comes with soft closure. The resulting tears of wonder, delight, and soft closure are the signs of those who dwell in the river's deep current.

When adults become conscious of the river's flow and eddies, they can speak about it, as we are doing here. Infants and children can't. They intuit how to find the river's deep current and express the quality of their involvement by laughter and tears. This is one reason why laughter and tears have been included in this description of the great river. The other reason is that sometimes laughter and tears is all adults can muster themselves to express what they know of God's creative energy.

I realize that this description of the creative process is very concentrated, but it is important to provide enough detail to suggest that your

---

THE INLAND DANGER ZONE:
This is where one can become stuck in chaos, where nothing is serious. Tears and laughter express madness.

ON THE RIVER BANK:
The openness of comedy is defined in opposition to the form of tragedy.

IN THE SHALLOWS OF THE FLOWING RIVER:
Creativity can be used for destructive as well as constructive ends.

THE DEEP CURRENT OF THE CREATIVE PROCESS

The creative process is wholly constructive and involves both the openness of comedy *and* the form of tragedy interacting.

The deep current has four dimensions: flow, play, love, and contemplation.

The 4 dimensions share 5 characteristics. The process is done for itself.
It is voluntary and involves deep concentration. It alters time, and is pleasurable.

The 5 steps in the process are the circle of: opening, scanning, insight, development, and soft closure.

The feelings aroused by the 5 steps are: wonder, curiosity, delight, careful caring, and satisfaction.
Tears and laughter express each step.

THE DEEP CURRENT OF THE CREATIVE PROCESS

IN THE SHALLOWS OF THE FLOWING RIVER:
Creativity can be used for destructive as well as constructive ends.

ON THE RIVER BANK:
The form of tragedy is defined in opposition to the openness of comedy.

THE INLAND DANGER ZONE:
This is where one can become stuck in rigidity, where everything is serious. Tears and laughter express scorn.

family, when it is at its best, is a living system that stores information, like the river, and yet is also flexible and flowing enough to communicate, create, and sustain life. The interplay of openness and structure, which supports creativity in children as well as adults is always available to help our families flourish, so this map is useful to help us find our true home as human beings.

The "maturity" of being in the deep channel is not the same as meeting the social norms of any particular culture. It is also not derived simply from accumulated age and experience although that may help us rediscover our deep identity. This kind of maturity, a maturity beyond the norm, can be found at any age, but, as Jesus said, children are especially significant for *showing* us how to enter this way of life (Matthew 19:13-15, Mark 10:13-16, Luke 18:15-17). They can show us how to live in God's kingdom without saying a word.

Our tendency, as human beings, is to move away from the deep current of the great river. We tend to lose touch with the Creator and allow the image of God within us to be obscured. Chaos spins apart our true self and rigidity grinds it down to diminish us as well as the creative community of our families, so we need to be alert.

The good news is that we can recover from evaporating on the barren banks of the great river. We can ask God for forgiveness and with God's help return to the graceful flow of the great river's deep current. One way to encourage this return is to begin where this book began. The annual renewing of our awareness of Creation, Christmas, Easter, Pentecost, the Good Shepherd, and the Liturgical Circle of the Year can help us recover our deep identity in the great river that flows out from and returns to God.

Conclusion

Let's conclude with a mostly nonverbal summing up. It draws from the images, movements, and words in the book's "storying" of God. Chapter 6 is especially relevant. You might get out the material for the church year or use your imagination to invoke it.

Move yourself around the circle by tracing it with your finger or your imagination to acknowledge God's creative flow, your personal creative circle, the circle of the liturgical year, and the circle of your family's experiences of life and death. Stop for a moment and reflect on each of these circles and how they reinforce each other. Then dwell for a moment at the center of the circle with the Good Shepherd and let this center point expand beyond the circle's circumference.

The next step is to lie down on your back. Put everything out of your mind as much as you can, even how strange this summing up might seem.

The third step is to place your hands lightly on your chest. Let them rest there for a moment, then lift your arms up toward the heavens, as if you are reaching out to draw in the Creator. Place your hands again lightly on your chest, as if you have taken in all of God to connect with God's image within. Imagine your right hand as the structure of the creative process and your left hand as its openness. These gestures help move you into the deep channel of creative energy flowing out from and returning to God.

The next step is to extend your arms out to the side as far as possible, leaving your hands open and relaxed. See if you can begin to feel the creative energy of God flowing through you as it does through all of creation. You may feel this first in your hands but eventually your whole body will become sensitive to the great river flowing through you. Stay there as long as you like, attuned to God's creative power.

When you are ready to conclude, place your hands again lightly on your chest. Take a deep breath, then get up refreshed to be with your family, knowing that we are all in God and God is in us.

When all is said and done, then, *what do you do* when you don't know what to do about past, present, and future challenges? You begin by layering in the stories of God, then you go to your still point to re-center yourself in the circle of God that has no circumference. This center point is a place that is "still" in sound but not movement. It is where you can feel the flood of the great river of God's creativity, flowing out from and returning to God. Go there to find the creative power you need to meet the challenges that arise for you and your family!